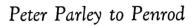

Peter Parley to Penrod

Peter Parley
to Penrod

A BIBLIOGRAPHICAL DESCRIPTION
OF THE BEST-LOVED AMERICAN
JUVENILE BOOKS

By

JACOB BLANCK

Editor of *Merle Johnson's American First Editions*
(3rd & 4th editions) ; *Bibliography of American Literature;*
compiler of *Harry Castlemon: Boys' Own Author;* etc., etc.,
and author of (for children) *Jonathan and the Rainbow*
and *The King and the Noble Blacksmith.*

MARK PRESS

WALTHAM, MASSACHUSETTS

1974

DEAR ALICE AND JOHN CORMAN:—Since it is to you
that this bibliography is dedicated it is no more than
reasonable that at the outset I should explain its pur-
pose. I know, and I hope that you don't think me pat-
ronizing, that you are far too young to find much interest in bibliography but some day you may become
curious about the books read by the Alices and by the
Johns that preceded both your generation and your god-
father's. When that time comes, and I am certain that
it will, perhaps this volume will be of some assistance.

Bookcollecting, in the purest form, is a matter of
sentiment, a sentiment so personal that it cannot be
measured or understood by any except those who find
a rare and satisfying pleasure in the possession of well-
loved volumes. And since bookcollecting is a sentimen-
tal manifestation what truer type of bookcollecting than
the gathering together of the books read as a child and
affectionately recalled? Certainly there is no period of
man's reading life more often remembered than the
first wondering years and the discovery of the strange

i

new worlds that are the printed page. You, Alice and John, cannot yet understand the nostalgic pleasure that is part of the possession of a collection of children's books. Nevertheless, as you come to your teens and later gain the dignity of the twenties, you too may find yourself reaching back in an effort to recapture the lost midsummer afternoons spent in adventuring with Huckleberry Finn or Tom Bailey.

First, I must tell you that in no sense is this selection offered with the suggestion that it is all-representative. Rather it is a list of those outstanding books which have withstood the years of change in reading tastes and are favorites still. Certain of the books are seldom read in these days but are included because of their position as milestones in juvenile reading during the past century. Too, this is an attempt to direct attention to certain books, once popular, that have been all but forgotten or overlooked and to furnish in broad strokes a picture of Young America's reading tastes. Your super-sophisticated collector friends may tell you that the essence of bookcollecting is rarity and that no book should be collected unless it is both rare and, to employ their over-used word, significant. You may tell such critics, Alice and John, that if rarity is to be the measure of selection, that Jacob Abbott's first title in the famed Rollo series, "Rollo Learning to Talk," is certainly rarer than "Tamerlane" if one may judge by the failure of bookhunters to locate a copy of the first edition. And as for significance . . . just consider the effect that Rollo or Fauntleroy had on not only juvenile fiction but the juvenile himself!

PREFACE

Since all books must be confined to the limits of their covers it has been impossible to include here all the works of the authors listed and for that reason I have tried to select the most most popular or the most representative work of each. But how is one to select Horatio Alger's most popular book? Or Oliver Optic's? In such cases it has seemed wise to describe the first title in a popular series and this method of selection has been followed. In the matter of selection I did not allow myself the luxury of acting as sole judge for if I had this bibliography would include in the first section such personal favorites as Edmund L. Pearson's "The Voyage of the Hoppergrass" and Clarissa Kneeland's "Smuggler's Island" . . . to say nothing of the entire contents of the buckram-bound file of *St. Nicholas* that I one day discovered (memorable day!) in an unlighted corner of the old Warren Street Branch of the Boston Public Library. This, then, must be my excuse and my apology to those who find that their personal favorites are not herein described. In making the final selection the following libraries, librarians and collectors registered their opinions as to what titles deserved inclusion in such a list: Carroll A. Wilson; John T. Winterich; Virginia Warren; Frank J. Hogan; Valta Parma of the Library of Congress, whose championship of the juvenile book has preserved for all time a magnificent collection for the people of the United States; Walter B. Briggs of Harvard University Library; Theodore Bolton, librarian of the Century Association, New York; Alice M. Jordan of the Boston Public Library; James I. Wyer of the New York State Library. If this bibliography included

all the favorites of American youth such books as "Rob-
inson Crusoe" and "Pinnocchio" would be present, but
this is a group of American products. True, you will
find listed certain authors—Burnett, Lofting and others
—who are not, in the strictest sense, Americans. But
these lived and worked on this side of the Atlantic and
may therefore be included in this work without further
explanation.

This bibliography is no attempt to trace the development of the American Juvenile except insofar as that
development is apparent in the list itself. The proper
province of the bibliographer is to record the physical
facts as they are, leaving to the scholar the task of
literary evaluation. Literary quality has in no way been
a factor in the final selection.

With the exception of Palmer Cox's "The Brownies"
no poetry or rhyme is included in this bibliography.
Poetry, save for the small doses crammed into the
schoolboy, seems to hold no real place in the reading-
child's world. Publishers have issued, and continue to
publish, inviting collections of the individual poets and
specialized anthologies, but children do not often of
their own volition turn to poetry. It seems safe to state
that the Rollos and the Fauntleroys of the juvenile
world are the only exceptions to this sad rule and
almost any librarian will tell you that replacements because of wear are not too often required in the poetry
section. A close second to this juvenile aversion is the
autobiographical work. Few of these are popular and
those that succeed are of such exceptional stuff that they
continue in spite of the first person singular . . .

PREFACE

"Huckleberry Finn" and "The Story of a Bad Boy"
holding first place in the rank of the notable exceptions.
Known as I books when the editor was more interested
in *Tyler, Toby* than *Tyler, John,* there is little indication that the condition has altered in recent years.

In using this bibliography it will be well to remem-
ber that during the nineteenth century American publishers frequently issued books in several colors or types
of binding. Therefore, if in the following pages a book ✳
is described as in blue cloth and you should find a copy
in orange, you must not assume that your copy is incorrect or that the bibliography is in error. Nor must
you be too quick to believe that yours is a pre-issue, an
experimental state, a variant or any of the other desig-
nations so gleefully pounced upon by bibliophile and
bookseller alike. Without positive proof regarding such
features you had best consider the differences as the
ordinary part of nineteenth century publishing in America, nevertheless recognizing the comparative scarcity
of, for example, an "Autocrat of the Breakfast Table"
in red cloth as against copies in drab brown.

And now, Alice and John, before I post this letter
I must tell you that I was greatly assisted in the pro-
duction of this book by David A. Randall who, as bookseller and bibliographer, has been helpfully interested
since the work was first suggested by Frederic G. Mel-
cher; assisted, too, by the staff of G. A. Baker & Company; by the nameless ladies at the Warren Street
Branch of the Boston Public Library (the *old* branch,
now become a grocery); by Florence G. Erskine, Grace
Cunningham and Mary McLaughlin, to mention but

PREFACE

three of my friends at the old George Putnam School;
and by so many others, librarians, collectors and dealers,
to whom my apologies for not being more specific. And,
before I forget, my thanks to Octavo, the bookshop
kitten, who sits on my knee as I type this, pretending
that she is one of the lions that guard the entrance to
the New York Public Library.

JACOB BLANCK

New York
1937-8

NOTE TO THE SECOND PRINTING

On August 1, 1938, *Peter Parley to Penrod* was published. Five weeks
later it was completely out of print. Precisely why the book found so
immediate acceptance is a question I shall not attempt to explain, for
a student of such matters could perhaps prove my words quite wrong
and, to my discomfort, demonstrate that the book was accepted merely
for want of a better.

But whatever the reason for its acceptance *Peter Parley to Penrod*
has been out of print since September, 1938, and I am frequently
embarrassed (in a mild sort of way) by reports of copies selling for
six or seven times the original published price—which, I am assured by
Authorities, is really no less than the book is worth. I comment only
that such acclaim should be reserved for the finer stuff that passes
through the pilastered grandeur of the auction rooms.

During the past several years three (or is it four?) publishers have
suggested a reprint. It was only when, a few weeks ago, yet another copy
of the book sold at auction for a nonsensically high price that I became
convinced the publishers were correct and a reprint might well be found
acceptable.

Let it be noted that this is not a revision although I have taken the
opportunity to add a few comments and to eliminate a few errors. Let
it be noted also that the standards and requirements of Bibliography
have changed for the better since this compilation was first issued. By
current standards *Peter Parley to Penrod* is something less than a perfect
instrument; it was far from perfect in 1938. That it is now somewhat
improved is due in large part to those who, like the compiler, have
affection for the stuff about which bibliographies are made rather than
✳ for the relatively bloodless compilations that are bibliographies.

J. B.

Chestnut Hill, Massachusetts
June 24th, 1956

1827

SAMUEL GRISWOLD GOODRICH
(Peter Parley)

(1793–1860)

THE / TALES / OF / PETER PARLEY. / About / America. / [*rule*] / With Engravings. / [*rule*] / S. G. Goodrich. . . . Boston. / [*dotted rule*] / MDCCC-XXVII. [1827]

The only copy that has come to the attention of the editor is that in the collection of Harvard University. Rebound, it is obvious that a complete collation cannot be given. It is quite possible that the Harvard copy's illustrations were scrambled in the rebinding and for that reason no attempt is made to collate them. The rebinding is so tight that it is impossible to determine whether or not the pictures are inserted or integral parts of the text. At any rate the original sheets as preserved collate as follows: 2 fly leaves; title page [p. 1]; copyright notice [p. ii]; preface, pp. [iii]–iv; text, pp. [5]–142. The copy is trimmed but the original edges are apparently untouched. Page measures $5\frac{1}{8}'' \times 4\frac{3}{16}''$.

Received at the Library of Congress February 24, 1827.

1834 (?)

JACOB ABBOTT

(1803–1879)

ROLLO: LEARNING TO TALK, *Boston, 1834(?)*

The first of the Rollo series and apparently the rarest. Continued search has failed to discover a copy, the volume lacking in even the author's personal collection now preserved at Bowdoin College. It is believed that the volume was first published in 1834 but definite information is wanting. It is probable that in format it is similar to the volume collated below, the ninth title in the series.

ROLLO'S / TRAVELS. / by the / Author of Rollo Learning to Talk, to / Read, at Work, at Play, at School, / at Vacation, &c. / [*rule*] / Boston: / William Crosby and Company, / 118 Washington Street. / 1840.

Collation: end paper; blank [p. 1]; frontispiece [p. 2]; title page [p. 3]; copyright notice dated 1839 [p. 4]; notice [p. 5]; table of contents [p. 6]; text, pp. [7]–189; blank [p. 190]; end paper.

Bound in dark grey cloth, the sides identically blind-stamped with a double-rule border having floral ornaments at each inner corner. The front cover is gold-stamped at the center: Rollo's / Travels

All edges trimmed. Size of leaf, $6\frac{3}{16}'' \times 4''$.

The compiler has seen a blue-wrappered publication containing part six of "Rollo at Work." Judging by the advertisements it would appear that all the Rollo books were so issued but apparently after book publication.

In a letter dated June 5th, 1938, Rollo G. Silver, now compiling a bibliography of Jacob Abbott, writes: "The reason why we cannot locate an 1835 copy of 'Rollo Learning to Talk'

JACOB ABBOTT

is that no book with that title was published in that year. From the evidence before me, this is what happened: In 1833 Abbott published a book called 'The Little Philosopher.' In 1835 he published 'The Little Scholar Learning to Talk,' subtitled 'A Picture Book for Rollo'; no copy is listed in the Union Catalog in Washington. In 1835 he also published 'Rollo Learning to Read,' a copy with one leaf missing and probably rebound is in the Amy Lowell Collection at Widener. This became so popular that in 1839 he reprinted 'The Little Scholar' as 'Rollo Learning to Talk' . . . only known copy is in the Amy Lowell Collection.

"In the 'Little Scholar,' Rollo is only mentioned in the last paragraph. Thus, as far as the series of Rollo books is concerned, this could be called a fore-runner rather than a member of the series. Thus 'Rollo Learning to Read' is the first volume of the Rollo series and 'Rollo Learning to Talk' appears after 'Rollo at School.' "

Prof. Silver's further researches, published in *The Colophon, New Graphic Series*, No. 2, N. Y., 1939, confirm his earlier surmise (set forth above) and clarify the genesis of the *Rollo* books. Rollo made his début in *The Little Scholar Learning to Talk, a Picture Book for Rollo, by His Father*, Boston: John Allen and Co., 1835; reissued in 1839 as *Rollo Learning to Talk*. In the 1835 publication Rollo appears but briefly. The first book devoted wholly to Rollo was *Rollo Learning to Read*, Boston, 1835.

1851

SUSAN WARNER
(Elizabeth Wetherell)

(1819–1885)

THE / WIDE, WIDE WORLD. / by / Elizabeth
Wetherell. / In Two Volumes. / [*rule*] / [*seven line
quotation from Longfellow*] / [*rule*] / Volume I.
[II.] / New-York: / George P. Putnam, 155 Broadway. / [*rule*] / 1851.

Collation of Vol. I: yellow end paper; fly leaf; title page
[p. i]; copyright notice dated 1850 [p. ii]; table of contents,
pp. [iii]–iv; text, pp. [9]–360; fly leaf; yellow end paper.

Collation of Vol. II: yellow end paper; 2 fly leaves; title
page [p. i]; copyright notice dated 1850 [p. ii]; table of
contents, pp. [iii]–iv; text, pp. [3]–330; 2 fly leaves;
yellow end paper.

Noted in both blue and brown cloth. Uniformly stamped
with blind decorative stamping on all covers and with publisher's monogram at center of sides. Spines gold-stamped:
The Wide / Wide World / [*rule*] / Vol. 1. [2.] / [*series of
horizontal double-rules and four ornaments*] / Putnam. Rule
at top and bottom of spine.

All edges trimmed. Size of leaf, $7\frac{1}{4}'' \times 4\frac{7}{8}''$.

In the first-printed copies the folio at p. 157, Vol. I, and
the folio at p. 34, Vol. II, are misplaced and appear at the
inner portion of the page rather than at the fore-edge.

It has been asserted, but with no substantiation, that the
first copies of the book were issued with the date, 1850, on
the title page. It is agreed that the book was published some
time before Christmas, 1850, and reviews appear in *The Lit-*

SUSAN WARNER

erary World, VII, 1850, p. 524, December 28, 1850 and in
The New York Commercial Advertiser, December 18, 1850.
The Copyright Office records receipt in the Southern District
of New York, December 5, 1850, with a copy received at
Washington on December 14th. The book became an instan-
taneous success and within two years of first publication ran
into thirteen American editions and several English editions,
both pirated and authorized.

1852

NATHANIEL HAWTHORNE

(1804–1864)

A / WONDER-BOOK / FOR / GIRLS AND BOYS.
/ by / Nathaniel Hawthorne. / With Engravings by
Baker from Designs by Billings. / Boston: / Ticknor,
Reed, and Fields. / MDCCCLII. [1852]

Collation: yellow end paper; fly leaf; inserted frontispiece;
title page [p. i]; copyright notice dated 1851 [p. ii]; preface,
pp. [iii]–iv; table of contents, pp. [v]–vi; text, pp. [7]–
256; fly leaf; end paper.

Bound in several colors of cloth, the sides identically blind-
stamped with decorations. The spine is gold-stamped: [*floral
decoration*] / Wonder-Book / [*decorative rule*] / Hawthorne
/ [*decoration*] / Ticknor & Co. / [*decoration*]

All edges trimmed. Size of leaf, 6⅝″ × 4⅜″. Frontispiece
and six full-page illustrations inserted.

Received at the Library of Congress for copyright December 22, 1851.

1852

SUSAN WARNER
(Elizabeth Wetherell)

(1819–1885)

QUEECHY. / by / Elizabeth Wetherell, / Author of "The Wide, Wide World." / [*one line from the Guardian*] / [*publisher's ornament: the globe encircled by ribbon bearing the names of Cooper, Irving, Bryant, etc.*] / Volume I. [II.] / New York: / George P. Putnam, 10 Park Place. / M. DCCC. LII. [*1852*]

Collation of Vol. 1: buff end paper imprinted with publisher's advertisements; title page [p. 3]; copyright notice [p. 4]; table of contents, pp. [5]–6; note [p. 7]; blank [p. 8]; text, pp. [9]–410; publisher's advertisements, 5 leaves, numbered as follows: 1, 2, 3, 4, 2, 3, 4, 7, 8, 10; inserted fly leaf; end paper as described. The advertisements are part of the final signature.

Collation of Vol. 2: end paper, imprinted with publisher's advertisements; inserted fly leaf; title page [p. 1]; copyright notice [p. 2]; table of contents, pp. [3]–4; text, pp. [5]–396; inserted fly leaf; end paper as described.

Bound in several colors of cloth. The sides are identically blind-stamped with a border and with the publisher's monogram at the center. The spine is gold-lettered: Queechy. / by the Author / of the / Wide Wide / World. / 1 [2]   The preceding is enclosed in a gold-stamped outline shield with the volume number immediately below in a circle. At the foot of the spine, gold-stamped, is: Putnam.

All edges trimmed. Size of leaf, $7\frac{5}{16}''$ × $4\frac{7}{8}''$ full.

Received for copyright at the Library of Congress April 23, 1852.

SUSAN WARNER

The advertisements on the inner cover of the first volume list "Queechy" as No. III on Putnam's list of new publications, giving April 15 as date of publication. Copies exist with unprinted yellow end papers but since the type in the book proper is noticeably worn it seems to indicate that such copies are later. Copies of the first volume have also been noted with an inserted fly leaf preceding the title page.

1852

FRANCIS ROBERT GOULDING

(1810–1881)

Robert and Harold / or the / YOUNG MAROON-
ERS / on the / Florida Coast. / by F. R. Goulding.
/ [decorative rule] / Philadelphia: / William S. Mar-
tien, / No. 144 Chestnut Street. / 1852

Collation: yellow end paper [pp. i–ii]; fly leaf [pp. iii–
iv]; inserted folding map ". . . showing the explorations of
the Young Marooners."; title page [p. v]; copyright notice
[p. vi]; foreword, *History of this Book,* pp. vii–viii; table of
contents, pp. ix–xii; text, pp. 13–422; 2 fly leaves; end paper.

Bound in black cloth with gilt-stamped vignette of children,
bear, cauldron, etc., on the front cover. Both sides are identically blind-stamped with an ornamental border. The spine is
gilt-stamped: [rule] / The / Young / Marooners / [decora-
tion] / F. R. Goulding. / [vignette: tree, birds, boy with
gun] / [ornament] / [rule]

All edges trimmed. Size of leaf, $6\frac{9}{16}''$ × $4\frac{1}{8}''$. The book is
illustrated with six inserted full-page plates.

Sequel: "Marooner's Island; or, Dr. Gordon in Search of
His Children," *Philadelphia, 1869.*

Received at the Library of Congress for copyright January
11, 1853.

1853

NATHANIEL HAWTHORNE

(1804–1864)

TANGLEWOOD TALES, / FOR / GIRLS AND
BOYS; / Being / a Second Wonder-Book. / by /
Nathaniel Hawthorne. / With Fine Illustrations. /
Boston: / Ticknor, Reed, and Fields. / M DCCC LIII.
[1853]

Collation: yellow end paper, at which is bound 8 pp. of
publisher's advertisements; 2 fly leaves, the first of which is
inserted; engraved decorative title page [pp. 1–2] inserted;
title page [p. 3]; copyright notice [p. 4]; table of contents,
p. 5; blank [p. 6]; introductory, pp. 7–18; text, pp. 19–336;
inserted fly leaf; yellow end paper.

Bound in several colors of cloth. The sides are identically
stamped with a blind rule border, floriated ornament at each
inner corner, decorative medallion at the center. The spine is
gold-stamped with floriated oval in which is stamped: Tanglewood / Tales / [*rule*] / Hawthorne / [*in another floriated
oval:*] Illustrated / Ticknor & Co. [*at foot*].

All edges trimmed. Size of leaf, $6\frac{9}{16}''\times 4\frac{1}{4}''$. Inserted are
six full page illustrations.

In the earliest state of the inserted advertisements the first
page lists 9 titles by Thomas De Quincey; the second page
lists "Tanglewood Tales" as *In Press*. Later states of the advertisements have an added title in the De Quincey list and
announce "Tanglewood Tales" as *Just Out*; still later with the
price *88 cts*. The earliest copies of the book proper have the
stereotyper's slug at the foot of the copyright page; later, the
printer's slug. Also, the earliest printed copies have unbroken
type at p. 242.

Received at the Library of Congress August 25th, 1853.

1854

MARIA SUSANNA CUMMINS

(1827–1866)

THE / LAMPLIGHTER. / [*diamond-rule*] / Boston: / Published by John P. Jewett & Company. / Cleveland, Ohio: / Jewett, Proctor and Worthington. / 1854.

Collation: yellow end paper; inserted fly leaf; title page [p. 1]; copyright notice [p. 2]; blank [pp. 3–4]; text, pp. [5]–523; blank [p. 524]; fly leaf [pp. 525–526]; end paper.

Bound in cloth, several colors noted. The sides are identically blind-stamped with the publisher's monogram at the center and ornamental border. The spine is gold-stamped: The / Lamp / Lighter / [*vignette: the lamplighter*] / Jewett & Co.

All edges trimmed. Size of leaf, $7\frac{5}{8}''$ scant $\times$ $4\frac{7}{8}''$.

Received at the Library of Congress for copyright March 16, 1854.

1855

WILLIAM TAYLOR ADAMS
(Oliver Optic)

(1822–1897)

THE / BOAT CLUB; / or, / The Bunkers of Rippleton. / A Tale for Boys. / by / Oliver Optic. / Boston: / Brown, Bazin, and Company. / 1855.

Collation: glazed yellow end paper; inserted fly leaf; inserted frontispiece; title page [p. 1]; copyright notice dated 1854 [p. 2]; dedication, p. 3; blank [p. 4]; preface, pp. 5–6; table of contents, pp. 7–8; sub-title [p. 9]; blank [p. 10]; text, pp. 11–252; inserted fly leaf; glazed yellow end paper.

Bound in slate-purple cloth (possibly others) with the sides identically blind-stamped with an ornamental panel and publisher's monogram at the center. The spine is gold-stamped, lengthwise, with a row-boat seating twelve boys; on the side of the boat, in cover color: The Boat Club.

All edges trimmed. Size of leaf, $6\frac{11}{16}'' \times 4\frac{1}{4}''$. In addition to the frontispiece there are three full page plates, inserted.

1855

THOMAS BULFINCH

(1796-1867)

THE / AGE OF FABLE; / or, / Stories of Gods and Heroes. / by / Thomas Bulfinch. / [*four lines from Barry Cornwall*] / Boston: / Sanborn, Carter, and Bazin. / 1855.

Collation: yellow end paper; inserted fly leaf; blank [p. i]; frontispiece [p. ii]; title page [p. iii]; copyright notice [p. iv]; dedication [p. 1]; blank [p. 2]; preface, pp. 3–6; table of contents, pp. 7–9; blank [p. 10]; text, pp. 11–476; *Proverbial Expressions,* pp. 477–479; *Index of Names,* pp. 480–485; blank [p. 486]; advertisements for Bulfinch's "Hebrew Lyrics," one leaf, inserted, printed on recto only; fly leaf, inserted; yellow end paper.

Bound in cloth, several colors and types noted. In one state the sides are identically blind-stamped with an all-over lozenge-like decoration with ornamental centers. The spine is gold-stamped: [*Cupid and clouds vignette*] / The / Age of / Fable / [*vignette of Daphne*]   Another binding noted: vertically ribbed brown cloth common to the period with the sides blind-stamped with decorative figures. The spine is gold-stamped: The / Age of / Fable / [*rule*] / Bulfinch.

Copies may have one or two fly leaves inserted at the back. The frontispiece has been noted in two states: on lightly calendered paper inserted; and, on book stock as a conjugate of the title page.

All edges trimmed. Size of leaf $7\frac{1}{2}''$ full $\times$ $4\frac{7}{8}''$.

In the first state of the first edition the names of both printer and stereotyper appear on the copyright page.

Published sometime before December 25, 1855. Received at the Library of Congress October 29, 1855.

1859

THOMAS BULFINCH

(1796–1867)

THE / AGE OF CHIVALRY. / Part I. / King Arthur and His Knights. / Part II. / The Mabinogeon; or, Welsh Popular Tales. / by / Thomas Bulfinch, / Author of "The Age of Fable." / [*4 lines from Words-worth*] / [*rule*] / Boston: / Crosby, Nichols, and Company, / 117 Washington Street. / 1859.

Collation: yellow end paper; inserted fly leaf; fly leaf; inserted frontispiece; title page [p. i]; copyright notice dated 1858 [p. ii]; dedication [p. iii]; blank [p. iv]; preface, pp. [v]–vi; table of contents, pp. [vii]–viii; sub-title [p. ix]; blank [p. x]; text, pp. [13]–254; subtitle for *The Mabinogeon* [p. 255]; text of *The Mabinogeon*, pp. [257]–414; one leaf (2 pp.) publisher's advertisements; fly leaf, inserted; yellow end paper.

Bound in black cloth with identical blind-stamping on the sides: double rule border within which an arabesque floral design. The spine is gold-stamped at the top with a vignette of an angel holding the graal below which is stamped: Age / of / Chivalry / [*vignette: Sir Owain, the lion and the serpent*] / Crosby, Nichols & Co.   Enclosed by gilt border.

All edges trimmed. Size of leaf, $7\frac{7}{16}'' \times 4\frac{3}{4}''$. There are, including the frontispiece, six full page illustrations all of which are inserted.

It is to be noted that the pagination is faulty in the preliminary leaves, a hiatus occurring at pp. x–13. This feature has been noted in all examined copies of the first edition.

This book has been noted in four states with no known priority. The above is hereinafter referred to as *State A* but the designation is in no way intended to establish priority.

14

THOMAS BULFINCH

State B collates as the preceding but the illustrations are highly colored and illuminated, the plates bearing the imprint: *Printed in Oil Colors, by Holland & Moffitt, 16 Franklin St., Boston.* The binding is of embossed cloth (several types noted) with the sides identically blind-stamped with triple-rule border having a lozenge-like ornament at each inner corner and a medallion at the center. The latter has been noted in gold as well as blind-stamping; edges either bevelled or plain. The spine has a series of rules at top and bottom, either blind or in gold, and is gold-lettered: Age of / Chivalry Several types of end papers have been noted; all edges trimmed and may be unstained, gilt or red-stained.

State C collates as *State A* but does not have the Boston imprint, in its stead appears: Cincinnati, Ohio: / Rickey, Mallory, & Co. / 1859.   The end papers are brown coated on white but the covers are the same as those of *State A* and carry the Boston imprint at the foot of the spine. In this state occurs a different arrangement of the preliminary leaves which collate as follows: brown-coated on white end paper; inserted fly leaf; fly leaf; inserted frontispiece; title page, copyright notice on the verso dated 1858; preface, pp. [v]–vi; dedication, verso blank; table of contents, pp. [vii]–viii; sub-title, verso blank; text, pp. [13]– . . . etc.

All edges trimmed. Size of leaf, $7\frac{7}{16}'' \times 4\frac{1}{2}''$. This state is printed on paper appreciably thinner than that of *State A.*

State D has the Boston imprint, the plates are in color but without the *Holland & Moffitt* imprint. The error (*see below*) on the plate at p. 94 has been corrected and the folio now reads *84*; the error on the plate at p. 291 has been altered to read *29.* The type at p. 213 is unbroken. All edges gilt.

Examination discloses that while all four states were printed by *Metcalf and Company, Cambridge,* whose imprint appears at the foot of the copyright page, the earliest printed copies have undamaged type in several places throughout the book. The most noticeable break is in the last line of p. 213. States A, B and C have the following error in common: the illustration at p. 84 is numbered *94*; the illustration at p. 291 is numbered *219.*

Received at the Library of Congress January 1, 1859.

1860

EDWARD SYLVESTER ELLIS

(1840–1916)

SETH JONES; / or, the / Captives of the Frontier /
[*rule*] / by Edward S. Ellis. / [*rule*] / New York: /
Irwin P. Beadle and Company. / 141 William St.,
Corner of Fulton. [1860]

Collation: blank [p. i]; frontispiece [p. 2]; title page [p.
3]; copyright notice dated 1860 [p. 4]; text, pp. [5]–123;
blank [pp. 124–128].

Bound in orange paper wrappers lettered in black. The front
cover reads: Published Semi-Monthly. / 123 Pages.] / [*diamond-rule*] [Complete. / Beadle's / Dime Novels / [*dime*]
/ No. 8. / The Choicest Works of the Most Popular Authors.
/ [*double rule*] / Seth Jones; / or, the / Captives of the
Frontier. / [*rule*] / by Edward S. Ellis. / [*rule*] / New-
York: / Irwin P Beadle & Co., 141 William St. / General
Dime Book Publishers. / [*rule*] / [*copyright notice, three
lines, dated 1860*]   Wholly enclosed by double-rule border.

The inner front wrapper is headed: *Ready November 1st /
Another Thrilling Romance!*

Inner rear wrapper is headed: *Beadle's / Dime School Mel-
odist.*

Rear wrapper lists several of the Beadle series including the
"Song Books," seven listed; and the "Dime Novels," eight
listed, "Seth Jones" being the eighth.

The spine is lettered but unfortunately the only copy avail-
able the compiler of this list is badly worn at the spine but
from what remains it is likely that, printed sideways, the
legend reads: Beadle's Seth Jones Number 8.

EDWARD SYLVESTER ELLIS

All edges trimmed. Size of leaf, $6\frac{9}{16}''\times 4\frac{1}{2}''$ full.

Received at the Library of Congress November 10, 1860.

As a matter of interest it is here recorded that although the cover and title page agree as to title the first page of text is headed: "Seth Jones of New Hampshire; or, the Captives of the Frontier." It was under the latter title that the book was reissued by Dillingham, *New York* [1907] with a special introduction by the author.

1861

JANE ANDREWS

(1835–1887)

THE / SEVEN LITTLE SISTERS / WHO LIVE ON
/ THE ROUND BALL / THAT / FLOATS IN THE
AIR. / With Illustrations. / Boston: / Ticknor and
Fields. / M DCCC LXI. [1861]

Collation: yellow end paper; fly leaf, inserted; four blank
leaves, on the verso of the fourth is printed a publisher's advertisement for *New Holiday Books for the Young*; half-title,
verso blank; inserted decorative title page; title page, copyright notice dated 1860 on the verso; dedication, verso blank;
table of contents, verso blank; text, pp. 1–127; blank [p.
128]; fly leaf, inserted; yellow end paper.

Bound in several colors of cloth with blind and gold stamping. The front cover is gold-stamped: The / Seven / Little
Sisters / Who Live on the Round Ball / That Floats in the
[*on gold-stamped ribbon*] / Air. Wholly enclosed by a blind-
stamped double-rule border with ornaments at each inner
corner. The back cover is identically stamped but wholly in
blind. The spine is gold-stamped: [*rule*] / The / Seven /
Little / Sisters / [*decoration*] / Ticknor & Co.

All edges trimmed. Size of leaf, $6\frac{5}{8}''$ scant $\times$ $4\frac{15}{16}''$.

Inserted are eight full page illustrations.

Received for copyright at the Library of Congress December 15, 1860.

1863

ADELINE DUTTON TRAIN WHITNEY

(1824–1906)

FAITH GARTNEY'S GIRLHOOD. / by the Author of / "Boys at Chequassett." / "To Do My Duty in That State of Life to Which it Shall Please God to Call Me." / [*diamond-rule*] / Loring, Publisher, / 319 Washington Street, / Boston. / 1863.

Collation: yellow end paper; inserted fly leaf; title page [p. 1]; copyright notice [p. 2]; preface [p. 3]; blank [p. 4]; table of contents, pp. [5]–6; text, pp. [7]–348; inserted fly leaf; end paper.

Bound in plum colored cloth with an all-over blind-stamping of small octagons. Sides identically blind-stamped with a triple-rule border. Spine gold-stamped: [*decorative rule*] / Faith / Gartney's / Girlhood / [*decoration*] / Loring / [*decorative rule*].

All edges trimmed. Size of leaf $7\frac{7}{16}''\times4\frac{13}{16}''$.

1864

JOHN TOWNSEND TROWBRIDGE

(1827–1916)

CUDJO'S CAVE. / by / J. T. Trowbridge, / Author of "Neighbor Jackwood," "The Drummer Boy," etc. / Boston: / J. E. Tilton and Company. / 1864.

Collation: yellow end paper; inserted fly leaf; decorative half title, inserted; title page [p. 1]; copyright notice dated 1863 [p. 2]; table of contents, pp. 3–4; text, pp. [5]–502; *L'Envoy,* pp. 503–504; inserted fly leaf; yellow end paper.

Bound in several colors and types of cloth. The sides are identically blind-stamped with triple-rule blind border. The spine is gold-stamped with a decorative field on which, in cover color, is: Cudjo's / Cave

All edges trimmed. Size of leaf, 7″ × 4½″ scant.

In the earliest copies the first page (p. 3) of the table of contents lists 22 chapters and at p. 4 *L'Envoy* is properly listed as at p. 503. The table of contents was later reset and in the reset state the *L'Envoy* is listed incorrectly as at p. 504, the error persisting as late as the 1890 period. This feature is the exception to the usual bibliographical rule that the error is the indication of first printing.

The book has been noted on both thick and thin papers but thus far no definite claim can be made for either state. Also in the nature of an unanswered problem, is the spine stamping which occurs in several patterns or designs and with or without the author's name. While the compiler of this list has no positive information regarding this it is highly probable that the first state of the stamping does not include the author's name or any other indication of authorship.

Received at the Library of Congress February 1, 1864.

1864

REBECCA SOPHIA CLARKE
(Sophie May)

(1833–1906)

LITTLE PRUDY. / by / Sophie May. / [*rule*] / Boston: / Lee and Shepard, / (Successors to Phillips, Sampson & Co.) 1864.

Collation: end paper; fly leaf; inserted frontispiece; title page [p. 1]; copyright notice dated 1863 [p. 2]; dedication, p. 3; table of contents, p. 4; text, pp. 5–167; blank [p. 168]; inserted fly leaf; end paper. The end papers occur in various colors and textures.

Bound in various cloths. The sides are identically blind-stamped with a decorative border. The spine is gold-stamped with lettering in cover color: Little / Prudy / by / Sophie May / Lee & Shepard

All edges trimmed. Size of leaf, $5\frac{15}{16}'' \times 3\frac{13}{16}''$. The frontispiece and two full page illustrations in the text are inserted.

Received at the Library of Congress for copyright June 28, 1864.

1865

ISABELLA MacDONALD ALDEN
(Pansy)
(1841–1930)

HELEN LESTER / [*ornamental rule*] / by Pansy. / [*ornamental rule*] / [*quotation from Ps. xxxiv: 11, 2 lines*] / [*ornament*] / Cincinnati: / American Reform Tract and Book Society. / No. 28 West Fourth Street. / 1865.

Collation: peach-tinted end paper; inserted fly leaf; frontispiece, inserted; title page [p. 1]; copyright notice, undated [p. 2]; table of contents, p. 3; blank [p. 4]; note: *Premium Offered* . . . p. 5; blank [p. 6]; text, pp. 7–132; publisher's advertisements, pp. 1–6; 4 fly leaves, the last of which is inserted; end paper, as described.

Bound in black cloth. The sides are identically blind-stamped with the ornamental seal of the American Reform Tract and Book Society. The spine is gold-stamped with ornaments and a ribbon; on the latter, in cover color, is: Helen Lester.

All edges trimmed. Size of leaf $5\frac{3}{4}''\times3\frac{7}{8}''$ scant. In addition to the frontispiece there are two full page illustrations, inserted. Received at the Library of Congress January 4, 1865.

Also noted: a copy with the following imprint: Cincinnati: / Western Tract and Book Society, / No. 28 West Fourth Street. / [n.d.].   This state varies but slightly from the copy collated above and is apparently printed from the same plates or type. Since the address of both societies is the same it would appear that the American Reform Tract and Book Society was the parent organization and that the books may have been simultaneously issued. No positive evidence has been forthcoming but in any event the title is so scarce that either state is desirable.

1865

REBECCA SOPHIA CLARKE
(Sophie May)

(1833–1906)

Little Prudy Series. / [*rule*] / DOTTY DIMPLE. / by / Sophie May. / [*rule*] / Boston: / Lee and Shepard, / (Successors to Phillips, Sampson & Co.) / 1865.

Collation: yellow end paper; inserted fly leaf; inserted frontispiece; title page [p. 1]; copyright notice [p. 2]; dedication, p. 3; blank [p. 4]; table of contents [p. 5]; blank [p. 6]; text, pp. 7–176; inserted fly leaf; yellow end paper.

Bound in various colors of cloth. The sides are identically blind-stamped with a decorative border. The spine is gold-stamped with the lettering in cover color: [*decorative rule*] / Little / Prudy's / Dotty / Dimple / Lee & Shepard

All edges trimmed. Size of leaf, $5\frac{7}{8}''\times 3\frac{13}{16}''$. In addition to the frontispiece there all two full page plates; all inserted.

Received at the Library of Congress November 22, 1865.

1865

EDWARD EVERETT HALE

(1822–1909)

THE / MAN WITHOUT A COUNTRY. / [*publisher's seal*] / Boston: / Ticknor and Fields. / 1865.

Collation: title page [p. 1]; copyright notice [p. 2]; text, pp. [3]–23; blank [p. 24].

Bound in light terra-cotta colored wrappers trimmed to the size of the page. The front cover is textually the same as the title page but the seal is larger and the whole is enclosed by a single-rule box.

The inner front wrapper is headed: *Alfred Tennyson's Works*. Inner back wrapper is headed: *Tennyson's Enoch Arden*. Back wrapper is headed: *Our Young Folks*.

All edges trimmed. Size of leaf, $6\frac{9}{16}''$ full × $4\frac{1}{8}''$.

Copies have been noted with a publisher's "announcement" slip tipped in at the title page. Whether or not such copies were the first issued is not known and it is presumed that any copy that collates as above, whether with the slip or not, is first edition.

Appeared originally in the *Atlantic Monthly* for December 1863.

1866

MARY ELIZABETH MAPES DODGE

(1836–1905)

HANS BRINKER; [*initals in red*] / or, / the Silver Skates. / a Story of Life in Holland. / by M. E. Dodge, / Author of "The Irvington Stories." / illustrated by / F. O. C. Darley and Thomas Nast. / [*publisher's monogram in red*] / New York: / James O'Kane, 126 Nassau Street. / M. DCCCLXVI. [1866]

Collation: yellow end paper; 2 fly leaves; frontispiece on tinted paper, inserted; title page, copyright notice dated 1865 on the verso; dedication [p. 1]; blank [p. 2]; preface, pp. [3]–4; table of contents, pp. [5]–8, with list of 4 full page illustrations at p. 8; text, pp. [9]–347; blank [p. 348]; publisher's advertisements, 2 pp., (also noted with 4 pp.); fly leaf; end paper. The advertisements have been noted in at least three states but thus far no priority has been determined.

Issued in several colors of pebbled cloth. The sides are identically stamped with a blind-rule border and publisher's monogram gilt-stamped at the center. Edges bevelled. The spine is gold-stamped: Hans / Brinker. / James O'Kane   Blind rule at top and bottom.

All edges trimmed. Size of leaf, $7\frac{5}{16}''\times 4\frac{7}{8}''$ full.

Apparently the illustrations were inserted with utter disregard as to pagination; this same condition has been noted in a third edition published in 1867.

Received at the Library of Congress for copyright November 22, 1865.

1867

MARTHA FINLEY
(Martha Farquharson)
(1828–1909)

ELSIE DINSMORE. / by Martha Farquharson, / Author of "Annandale," "Allan's Fault," "Brookside Farm- / House," etc., etc. / [*4 lines from Moore's "Loves of the Angels"*] / New York: / M. W. Dodd, 605 Broadway. / 1867.

Collation: manila-yellow end paper; fly leaf; frontispiece, recto blank [pp. 1–2]; decorative title page, verso blank [pp. 3–4]; title page [p. 5]; copyright notice [p. 6]; text, pp. [7]–288; fly leaf; end paper as described.

Bound in cloth, red noted. Sides identically blind-stamped with double-rule border and circular floral decoration at the center. Spine gold-stamped: Elsie / Dinsmore [the two lines preceding enclosed in a box, floriated at top and bottom] / M. W. Dodd. Gold rules at top and bottom of spine.

But two copies of this volume have come to the compiler's attention; both have the publisher's address on the title page as *605* Broadway and *506* on the decorative title page. The publisher's correct address was 506 Broadway but whether or not copies of "Elsie Dinsmore" were issued with the corrected title page is not known.

All edges trimmed. Size of leaf, $6\frac{1}{2}''\times 4\frac{3}{8}''$.

1867

CHARLES AUSTIN FOSDICK
(Harry Castlemon)

The Gun-Boat Series. / [*rule*] / FRANK / ON THE LOWER MISSISSIPPI. / by / Harry Castlemon, / "The Gun-Boat Boy." / [*rule*] / With Illustrations. / [*rule*] / Cincinnati: / R. W. Carroll & Co., Publishers, / 117 West Fourth Street. / 1867.   Wholly enclosed by single-rule box.

Collation: brown-coated on white end paper; 2 fly leaves; decorative title page [pp. i–ii]; blank [p. iii]; list of books in the "Gun Boat Series," five titles listed [p. iv]; title page [p. v]; copyright notice [p. vi]; table of contents, pp. vii–viii; text, pp. 9–236; 3 fly leaves; end paper, as described.

Bound in various colors of cloth with identical blind-stamping on the sides: triple-rule border and publisher's monogram at center. Spine gold-stamped: Frank / on the / Lower / Mississippi / Gun-Boat Series [*enclosed in oval*] / R. W. Carroll & Cᵒ / Cincinnati   Spine further decorated with gold-stamped moose-head, oars, steamboat, etc.

All edges trimmed. Size of leaf, $6\frac{3}{4}''$ scant × $4\frac{5}{8}''$.

Received at the Library of Congress July 29, 1867.

1868

PAUL BELLONI DU CHAILLU

(1831–1903)

STORIES / OF THE / GORILLA COUNTRY. / Narrated for Young People. / by Paul Du Chaillu, / Author of "Discoveries in Equatorial Africa," etc., etc. / With Numerous Illustrations. / New York: / Harper & Brothers, Publishers, / Franklin Square. / 1868.

Collation: brown-coated on white end paper; fly leaf, inserted; frontispiece [pp. i–ii]; title page [p. iii]; copyright notice dated 1867 [p. iv]; table of contents, pp. [v]–ix; blank [p. x]; list of illustrations, pp. [xi]–xii; text, pp. [13]–292; publisher's advertisements, 2 leaves (4 pp.); inserted fly leaf; end paper, as described.

Bound in several colors of cloth with gold stamping. The front cover is stamped with the title in cover color on a gold-stamped ribbon: Stories / of / the / Gorilla Country / [*vignette: a gorilla*] / by / Paul Du Chaillu   The cover is bordered by a single-rule box. The spine is gold stamped with all lettering in cover color: Stories / of the / Gorilla / Country / -o- / P. Du Chaillu / Numerous / Illustrations / Harpers The spine is gold-stamped with jungle decorations of snake, crane, vegetation, etc. The back cover is blind-stamped at the center with publisher's seal and single-rule border. Edges of the cover are bevelled.

All edges trimmed. Size of leaf, $7\frac{3}{8}'' \times 4\frac{15}{16}''$. All illustrations as listed are integral parts of the book.

Received for copyright at the Library of Congress January 3, 1868.

1868

HORATIO ALGER, Jr.

(1834–1899)

RAGGED DICK; / or, / Street Life in New York / With the Boot-Blacks. / by / Horatio Alger, Jr., / Author of "Frank's Campaign," "Paul Prescott's Charge," "Charlie / Codman's Cruise," "Helen Ford." / [*decorative rule*] / Loring, Publisher, / 319 Washington Street, / Boston. [1868]

Collation: tinted end paper; inserted fly leaf; blank [p. i]; list of Alger's books [p. ii] with "Fame and Fortune" announced for publication *In December*; inserted decorative title page; title page [p. iii]; copyright notice dated 1868 [p. iv]; dedication [p. v]; blank [p. vi]; preface, pp. vii–viii; text, pp. 9–296; inserted fly leaf; end paper, as described.

Bound in several colors of cloth. The front and back covers are identically blind-stamped with a decorative border and an ornament at the center. The spine is gold-stamped: Ragged / Dick / [*vignette of Dick*] /   The spine is further stamped with a rule box, decorative rules and interlocking double-rules under the title.

All edges trimmed. Size of leaf, $6\frac{3}{4}'' \times 4\frac{1}{2}''$.

The story was first published serially in *Student and School-mate* (Boston) January 1867 to December 1867, inclusive. Received for copyright at the Library of Congress May 20, 1868.

1868

LOUISA MAY ALCOTT

(1832–1888)

LITTLE WOMEN / or, / Meg, Jo, Beth and Amy / by Louisa M. Alcott / Illustrated by May Alcott / Boston / Roberts Brothers / 1868

Collation: brown-coated on white end paper; inserted frontispiece; title page [p. i]; copyright notice [p. ii]; table of contents, pp. [iii]–iv; preface [p. v]; blank [p. vi]; text, pp. 7–341; blank [p. 342]; three leaves (6 pp.) of publisher's advertisements numbered 3, 2, 11, 12, 8, 11; inserted fly leaf; end paper, as described. The advertisements are an integral part of the last signature.

Bound in cloth, several colors noted. The front cover is gold-stamped at the center: Little / Women / [*diamond-rule*] / L. M. Alcott   The lettering is enclosed by an upright double-rule oval containing within the rules a conventionalized sea-wave design. The edge of the cover is bordered by a blind-stamped double-rule. The spine is gold-stamped with the same oval-enclosed lettering of the front cover; at the bottom is gold-stamped: Boston / Roberts Bros. / Ornamental rule at top and bottom of spine. Back cover blind-stamped with double-rule border.

All edges trimmed. Size of leaf, $6\frac{9}{16}$" scant $\times$ $4\frac{3}{8}$". All the illustrations (four, including the frontispiece) are separately printed and inserted.

The first state of the first edition does not have an announcement of "Little Women, Part Two," at the foot of the last page of text, nor does *Part One* appear on the spine.

Received at the Library of Congress October 3, 1868.

1869

ELIJAH KELLOGG

(1813–1901)

Elm Island Stories. / [*rule*] / LION BEN / OF / ELM ISLAND. / by / Rev. Elijah Kellogg, / Author of "Spartacus to the Gladiators," / "Good Old Times," etc. / Boston: / Lee and Shepard. / 1869.

Collation: yellow end paper; fly leaf; inserted frontispiece; inserted engraved title page; title page [p. 1]; copyright notice dated 1868 [p. 2]; list of "Elm Island Stories," two titles listed [p. 3]; blank [p. 4]; preface, pp. 5–6; table of contents, pp. 7–8; text, pp. 9–265; blank [p. 266]; 6 pp. publisher's advertisements; inserted fly leaf; end paper, as described.

Bound in several colors of cloth. The sides are identically blind-stamped with a double-rule border. Spine is gold-stamped: Lion / Ben' /Elm Island /Stories / Lee & Shepard The spine is further decorated with scrolls, leaves, animal head, etc.

All edges trimmed. Size of leaf $6\frac{5}{8}'' \times 4\frac{1}{4}''$. Frontispiece and two full-page illustrations are inserted.

1870

FRANK (FRANCIS RICHARD) STOCKTON

(1834–1902)

TING A LING / by / Frank R Stockton. / Illustrated by / E. B. Bensell / New York: / Hurd and Houghton, / Riverside Press Cambridge, / 1870   The entire title page is hand-drawn and lettered, the lettering being an integral part of the decorations consisting of a scene in which several of the book's characters are participants.

Collation: glazed yellow end paper; fly leaf; title page, copyright notice dated 1869 on verso; dedication, verso blank; text, pp. 1–187; blank [p. 188]; fly leaf; end paper.

Bound in several colors of cloth with black and gold stamping. The front cover is gold-lettered: Ting-a-Ling / Frank R. Stockton   Black-stamped between the two lettered lines is a door-like panel with decorative peacock feathers in gold at the center. The back cover is stamped with the same door-like ornament in black. The spine is lettered in gold, sideways, reading from top to bottom: Ting-a-Ling There is a black-stamped ornament at each end of the lettered line. Edges of cover bevelled.

All edges trimmed. Size of leaf, $7\frac{11}{16}'' \times 5\frac{5}{8}''$. All illustrations are integral parts of the text.

Portions of the text appeared in the *Riverside Magazine*, November and December, 1867; February and July, 1869. Received at the Library of Congress February 23, 1870.

1870

LOUISA MAY ALCOTT

(1832–1888)

AN OLD-FASHIONED GIRL. / by / Louisa M. Alcott, / Author of "Little Women." / With Illustrations. / Boston: / Roberts Brothers. / 1870.

Collation: brown-coated on white end paper; inserted fly leaf; one sheet folded to make four pages, on the verso of the first a picture of *Tom*, on the recto of the second a picture of *Polly*; title page, copyright notice on the verso; one leaf, recto blank, verso imprinted with publisher's advertisements for "Little Women" and "Hospital Sketches."; preface [p. 1]; blank [p. 2]; index, pp. [3]–4; text, pp. [1]–378; publisher's advertisements, pp. [1]–8; inserted fly leaf; end paper. P. [2] of the advertisements is dated March, 1870.

Bound in cloth, <u>several colors</u> noted. At the center of the front cover is gold-stamped: Old- / Fashioned / Girl / [*diamond-rule*] / L. M. Alcott   The lettering is enclosed by an upright oval containing within the rules a conventionalized sea-wave design. The spine is gold-stamped with the same oval-enclosed lettering of the front cover; at the foot of the spine, in gold: Boston / Roberts Bros.   At top and bottom of spine, also gold-stamped, is an ornamental rule. Both front and back covers are bordered by a blind-stamped double-rule.

All edges trimmed. Size of leaf, $6\frac{9}{16}''\times 4\frac{3}{8}''$. In addition to the two illustrations preceding the title page there is an illustration inserted at p. 333 and one at p. 371.

Noted in three variant states as follows:
First: As collated above, with no advertisements on the copyright page. At p. 159, line 17, the word *at* is repeated.
Second: The advertisements appear on the copyright page, and not on a separate leaf as in the preceding state. The typographical error at p. 159 remains uncorrected.

Third: The advertisements appear on the copyright page and the typographical error at p. 159 has been corrected.

Copies have been noted with paper label on the spine but the status of such copies has not been determined.

Received for entry at the Library of Congress April 20, 1870.

1870

THOMAS BAILEY ALDRICH

(1836–1907)

THE / STORY OF A BAD BOY / by / Thomas
Bailey Aldrich. / With Illustrations. / [*publisher's
monogram*] / Boston: / Fields, Osgood, & Co. / 1870.

Collation: brown-coated on white end paper; inserted fly
leaf; inserted frontispiece; title page [p. i]; copyright notice
dated 1869 [p. ii]; table of contents, pp. [iii]–iv; list of illustrations [p. v]; blank [p. vi]; text, pp. [7]–261; blank
[p. 262]; fly leaf; publisher's advertisements, pp. 1–23, verso
of the latter [p. 24], blank; inserted fly leaf; end paper, as
described.

Bound in cloth, several colors noted. Front and back covers
are identically blind-stamped with an ornamental border. The
spine is gold-stamped with two vignettes and lettered: The /
Story of a / Bad Boy / by / T. B Aldrich / Illustrated /
Fields, Osgood & Co / Spine bordered by single-rule box.

All edges trimmed. Size of leaf, $7'' \times 4\frac{1}{2}''$. Of the illustrations listed at [p. v] two, including the frontispiece, are
inserted; the others are textual.

The first state of the first edition is distinguished by the
following typographical errors: p. 14, line 20, *scattered* for
scatters; p. 197, line 10, *abroad* for *aboard*. In addition to
the regularly issued trade edition as here collated there is a
large paper state of which there are said to have been but six
copies printed. It is further stated that of this large paper
edition three were destroyed by fire.

The story was first published serially in *Our Young Folks*,
January 1869 to December 1869, inclusive. The Library of
Congress states that the book was received for copyright "prob-
ably before Christmas, 1869."

1871

LOUISA MAY ALCOTT

(1832–1888)

LITTLE MEN: / Life at Plumfield with Jo's Boys. / by / Louisa M. Alcott, / Author of "Little Women," "An Old-Fashioned Girl," / "Hospital Sketches." / [*decoration*] / Boston: / Roberts Brothers. / 1871.

Collation: brown-coated on white end paper; fly leaf; four pages of publisher's advertisements, "Pink and White Tyranny" at the last page announced as *Nearly Ready*; inserted frontispiece; title page, copyright notice on verso; dedication, table of contents on verso; text, pp. 1–376; fly leaf; end paper, as described.

Bound in cloth, several colors noted. The front cover is gold-stamped at the center: Little / Men / [*rule*] / L. M. Alcott   The lettering is enclosed by an upright double-rule oval containing within the rules a conventionalized sea-wave design. The spine is gold-stamped: [*decorative rule*] / [*here is repeated the oval-enclosed lettering of the front cover*] / Boston / Roberts Bros / [*decorative rule*]   Both front and back covers are bordered by a blind-stamped double-rule.

All edges trimmed. Size of leaf, $6\frac{9}{16}''$ × $4\frac{3}{8}''$. Including the frontispiece there are four full page illustrations, printed separately and inserted.

Received for copyright at the Library of Congress June 12, 1871.

1871

HORATIO ALGER, Jr.

(1834–1899)

TATTERED TOM; / or, / the Story of a Street Arab. / by / Horatio Alger, Jr., / Author of "Ragged Dick Series," "Luck and Pluck Series," / "Campaign Series." / [*decorative rule*] / Loring, Publisher, / Cor. Bromfield and Washington Streets, / Boston. [1871]

Collation: yellow end paper; fly leaf, inserted; publisher's advertisements [pp. i–ii] printed on verso only, the last item being "Paul, the Peddler" announced for publication in *November, 1871*; inserted frontispiece; inserted decorative title page; title page, copyright notice on the verso dated 1871 [pp. iii–iv]; dedication [p. v]; blank [p. vi]; preface, pp. vii–viii; text, pp. [9]–282; publisher's advertisements, 4 pp.; fly leaf; inserted fly leaf; yellow end paper.

Bound in several colors of cloth. Front and back covers identically blind-stamped with decorative border and ornament at center. Spine is gold-stamped: [*decorative rule*] / Tattered / Tom /Tattered Tom / Series / [*vignette of crossing-sweeper*] / [*decorative rule*]   Title is enclosed in a decorative box; the series title appears in cover color on a gold-stamped field.

All edges trimmed. Size of leaf, $6\frac{3}{4}'' \times 4\frac{1}{2}''$.

The frontispiece, decorative title page and two full page illustrations in the text are inserted.

Received at the Library of Congress for copyright August 12, 1871.

1871

JOHN TOWNSEND TROWBRIDGE

(1827–1916)

JACK HAZARD / AND HIS FORTUNES. / by / J. T. Trowbridge, / Author of "Coupon Bonds," "Lawrence's Adventures," / etc. / [*publisher's monogram*] / Boston: / James R. Osgood and Company, / Late Ticknor & Fields, and Fields, Osgood, & Co. / 1871.

Collation: brown-coated on white end paper; fly leaf; frontispiece, inserted; title page [p. i]; copyright notice [p. ii]; table of contents, pp. [iii]–iv; text, pp. 1–254; 2 fly leaves; end paper as described.

Bound in several colors of cloth. The sides are identically blind-stamped with a decorative border. The spine is gold-stamped with the title in cover color: Jack / Hazard / and / His Fortunes / [*vignette of dog*] / James R. Osgood & Co The spine is decorated with an elaborate gold-stamped design. The publisher's name is gold-stamped.

All edges trimmed. Size of leaf 7″ × 4½″.

Appeared serially in *Our Young Folks,* January to December, 1871. Received at the Library of Congress November 10, 1871.

1873

SARAH CHAUNCEY WOOLSEY
(Susan Coolidge)

(1835–1905)

WHAT KATY DID. / a Story. / by / Susan Coolidge, / Author of "The New-Year's Bargain." / [rule] / With Illustrations by Addie Ledyard. / [rule] / Boston: / Roberts Brothers. / 1873.

Collation: brown-coated on white end paper; fly leaf; frontispiece, inserted; title page [p. i]; copyright notice dated 1872 [p. ii]; *To Five,* pp. iii–iv; table of contents, pp. v–vi; text, pp. 7–274; publisher's advertisements, 2 pp.; fly leaf; end paper, as described.

Issued in several colors of pebbled cloth. The front cover is gold-lettered: What / Katy Did   Further stamped with a cat-o'-nine-tails in black and a grasshopper in gold; the lettering is bisected vertically with a gold-stamped cat-o'-nine-tails with a grasshopper on one leaf. The spine is gold-stamped: What / Katy / Did / Susan Coolidge [*all of preceding in individual decorative boxes*] / [*publisher's monogram*]

All edges trimmed. Size of leaf, $6\frac{13}{16}''$ × $4\frac{7}{8}''$.

Received at the Library of Congress January 7, 1874.

1874

CHARLES ASBURY STEPHENS

(1847–1931)

THE / YOUNG MOOSE HUNTERS, / A Backwoods-Boy's Story. / by / C. A. Stephens. / Author of "The Camping Out Series." / Illustrated by Merrill. / [*publisher's device*] / Boston: / Henry L. Shepard & Co., / (Late Shepard & Gill) / 1874.

Collation: yellow end paper; inserted fly leaf; frontispiece [pp. 1–2]; title page [p. 3]; copyright notice [p. 4]; table of contents, pp. 5–6; text, pp. [7]–228; inserted fly leaf; end paper.

Bound in green cloth, stamped in black and gold. The front cover is stamped in black with the following in cover-color: American Homes Series   *H* in *Homes* is black-stamped. The line of lettering circles the upper portion and sides of a gold-stamped vignette of a moose-hunting scene below which is lettered in cover color on a black field: The Young Moose Hunters   At the bottom of the cover, in black, is: C. A. Stephens   The front cover is decorated with black-stamped rules and ornaments. The spine is gold and black-stamped. Gold lettered: The / Young / Moose / Hunters / American Homes / Series / [*the following in cover color on gold:*] H. L. Shepard & Co.   The spine is further decorated with rules and ornaments in black and gold and a gold-stamped vignette of two moose-hunters.

All edges trimmed. Size of leaf, $7\frac{3}{8}''$ full $\times$ $5\frac{5}{16}''$.

Received at the Library of Congress January 29, 1875.

1875

HORACE ELISHA SCUDDER

(1838–1902)

DOINGS / OF THE / BODLEY FAMILY / IN
TOWN AND COUNTRY / by the Author of /
"Stories From My Attic," "Dream Children," and
"Seven Little People / and Their Friends" / With
Seventy-Seven Illustrations / [*circular vignette: basket,
pitcher, pitchforks, etc.*] / New York / Published by
Hurd and Houghton / Cambridge: The Riverside Press
/ 1875

Collation: drab-brown-coated on white end paper printed
with a series of black silhouettes; inserted fly leaf; blank [p.
i]; frontispiece [p. ii]; title page [p. iii]; copyright notice
[p. iv]; dedication [p. v]; blank [p. vi]; table of contents,
pp [vii]–viii; text, pp. [9]–250; publisher's advertisements,
pp. [1]–4; fly leaf; end paper, as described.

Bound in blue cloth. Apparently the edges of the covers are
(to borrow a term from the Ladies) piped rather than bound
and over the boards are pasted black-lettered sheets of gray
paper. On the front cover the sheet-printing is: Doings of the
Bodley / Family in Town / and Country / [*vignette: 3
children at the foot of a sugar-maple*] / The Riverside Press
[*enclosed in a single-rule box, the horizontal lines extending
beyond the vertical*]   On the back cover the sheet is printed
at the upper left with a vignette of a fairy and some other
nameless creature out of the fairy-tales. At the lower portion
of the sheet is printed a note beginning: *This book was written
for the amusement of children. It contains* . . . There is also
an arrangement of three rules. The spine is stamped in gold
and black: Doings [*in gold, accented in black*] / of the [*in
black, accented in gold*] / Bodley / Family [*the 2 preceding
lines are in black on a gold field*] / [*black floral decoration*

with gold-stamped bird and fox] / Hurd & Houghton [*in gold*] /   The spine is further decorated with rules and ornaments in gold and black.

All edges trimmed. Size of leaf, $8\frac{1}{8}''\times 6\frac{1}{2}''$ full. All illustrations are integral parts of the book.

Much of the material, as explained by the author at p. viii, is the work of authors other than Scudder and he gives credit to Mrs. A. D. T. Whitney and to a Miss Annette Bishop. Two of the original Bodley stories, however, have been located in *The Riverside Magazine* for April and July, 1867.

Received at the Library of Congress October 15, 1875.

1876

SAMUEL LANGHORNE CLEMENS
(Mark Twain)

(1835–1910)

THE ADVENTURES / OF / TOM SAWYER / by
/ Mark Twain. / [*rule*] / The American Publishing
Company, / Hartford, Conn.: Chicago, Ill.: Cincinnati,
Ohio. / A. Roman & Co., San Francisco, Cal. / 1876.

Collation: brownish-yellow end paper; 2 (or 3) fly leaves;
half title [p. i]; blank [p. ii]; blank [iii]; frontispiece [p.
iv]; title page [p. v]; copyright notice dated 1875 [p. vi];
dedication [p. vii]; blank [p. viii]; preface [p. ix]; blank
[p. x]; table of contents, pp. [xi]–xiii; blank [p. xiv]; list
of illustrations, pp. [xv]–xvi; text, pp. [17]–274; conclusion
[p. 275]; blank [p. 276]; publisher's advertisements [pp.
277–280]; 2 (or 3) fly leaves; end paper, as described.

Note: the fly leaves are of laid paper unlike the stock on
which the book is printed. The number varies and thus far no
study of the book reveals a preferred state. It would appear
that the number of leaves was dependent wholly upon the
whim of the individual binder, a questionable quantity that
cannot be analyzed.

Issued, simultaneously it is presumed, in various types of
leather and in blue cloth. Cloth copies are stamped as follows
in gold and black. Front cover: Adventures [*in cover color
on gold field. Below this, in gold:*] of / Tom Sawyer.   Further decorated with gold and black stamping of rules, boxes,
circles, scrolls, etc. I have noted a copy of the 1877 printing
with two sunburst medallions instead of the usual gold-
stamped stars at the sides. Spine is stamped: Adventures / of
/ Tom Sawyer [*the three preceding lines are in cover color on
a gold field. Below this, in cover color on a gold field:*] by
Mark Twain. / [*the following in gold:*] Am. Pub. Co.

The spine is further decorated with a series of rules and decorations in black-stamping. At the center of the back cover is the black-stamped publisher's monogram. At top and bottom, extending the entire width, is stamped a horizontal decorative rule. These rules have been noted in varying positions as to the unit of decoration at the fore-edge and it has been asserted that only in the earliest copies is the unit unbroken. As opposed to this theory, however, is the fact that editions issued in later years have the horizontal decorative rules in both varying states.

All edges trimmed. Size of leaf, $8\frac{3}{8}$" $\times$ $6\frac{1}{2}$". Copies were also issued with all edges gilt.

In the first state of the first edition the half-title, as collated above, is printed on a separate leaf. In later printings the half-title appears on the reverse of the frontispiece. Printed on calendered paper, the first state measures but 1" across the top of covers; later printed on an appreciably thicker paper. The earliest printed copies have perfect type, last line of the first page of text and at the last lines of p. 202. A complete bibliographical discussion of this title appears in the late Merle Johnson's "A Bibliography of Mark Twain," *New York*, 1935.

The book was published during December 1876 although application for copyright had been made as early as July 21, 1875; copies were not received for entry at the Library of Congress until January 2, 1877. The English edition was published on June 9, 1876, about six months before the American edition was put on sale. It is claimed that a pirated edition was printed and published in Canada and preceded the American edition in time of publication; this is not improbable but it is almost certain that the Canadian edition did not precede the English.

1876

JOHN HABBERTON

(1842–1921)

HELEN'S BABIES. / With / Some Account of Their Ways Innocent, Crafty, / Angelic, Impish, Witching, and Repulsive. / Also, / A Partial Record of Their Actions During Ten Days / of Their Existence. / by / Their Latest Victim. / [*decorative rule*] / Loring, Publisher, / Cor. Bromfield & Washington Streets, / Boston. / [1876]

Collation: title page [p. 1]; copyright notice dated 1876 [p. 2]; dedication [p. 3]; blank [p. 4]; text, pp. [5] 206; publisher's advertisements [pp. 207–208].

Bound in black-printed grey paper wrappers. The front cover is lettered: Loring's Tales of the Day. / [*double-rule*] / Helen's Babies. / With / Some Account of Their Ways, Innocent, / Crafty, Angelic, Impish, Witching, / and Repulsive. / Also, / a Partial Record of their Actions during Ten Days of their Existence. / by / Their Latest Victim. / Loring, Publisher, / Corner Bromfield and Washington streets, / Boston. / Price, 50 Cents.

The inside of the front wrapper lists three titles, the first being "How I Managed My Home on £200 a Year." Inside of the back cover imprinted with publisher's advertisements, the first book listed being "Zerub Throop's Experiment." The back cover is occupied with an advertisement for "Helen's Babies." The spine is lettered sideways, reading from top to bottom: Helen's Babies.

The single leaf of publisher's advertisements is headed at [p. 207]: *Books for Young Ladies;* [p. 208] is headed: *Loring's Standard English Novels.*

45

Printed on laid paper. All edges trimmed, size of leaf $6\frac{9}{16}''$ $\times$ $5\frac{3}{16}''$.

The first state of the first edition collates as above. There exists also a later state printed from the same metal but the book is appreciably thinner (measures about $\frac{1}{2}''$ thick as against the first edition thickness of $\frac{13}{16}''$) and is on wove paper. The first state has perfect type at p. 13 and at the right margin of p. 188; in the later states the type at these pages is broken. The advertisements in the later state differ from those of the first edition, the inside front wrapper carrying the publisher's advertisement for "Pique." I have seen no copy bound in cloth that can be safely called a first printing of the book. Since early advertisements for the title list paper binding only and have no mention of cloth it is almost certain that the first edition was issued in wrappers only.

1877

CHARLES CARLETON COFFIN
("Carleton")
(1823–1896)

THE BOYS OF '76. / a History of / the Battles of
the Revolution. / by Charles Carleton Coffin, / Author
of / "My Days and Nights on the Battle-Field," "Following the Flag," "Four Years of / Fighting," "Win-
ning his Way," "Our New Way Round the World,"
&c. / Illustrated. / [*publisher's seal*] / New York: /
Harper & Brothers, Publishers, / Franklin Square. /
1877.

Collation: brown-coated on white end paper; fly leaf; fly
leaf [pp. 1–2]; frontispiece [pp. 3–4]; title page [p. 5];
copyright notice dated 1876 [p. 6]; dedication [p. 7]; blank
[p. 8]; preface [p. 9]; blank [p. 10]; table of contents, pp.
[11]–12; list of illustrations, pp. [13]–16; text, pp. [17]–
398; 2 fly leaves; end paper, as described.

Bound in cloth, mauve and blue noted, stamped in gold
and black. Lettered in gold on the front cover: The Boys
/ of '76   Decorated further with gold-stamping: head of
Colonial soldier, scrolls, drum, eagle, etc. Also black-stamped
decorations of rules, boxes, floral decorations, etc. The spine
is stamped: [*black decorative box*] / The / Boys / of / '76 /
[*decoration*] / Charles C. Coffin / [*decoration*] / Harper /
& / Brothers / [*black decorative box*] /   The spine is
gold-stamped except as noted. The back cover is blind-stamped
with decorative boxes at top and bottom and publisher's monogram at the center.

All edges trimmed. Size of leaf, $8\frac{13}{16}'' \times 6\frac{7}{16}''$.

Received at the Library of Congress November 15, 1876.

1877

NOAH BROOKS

(1830–1903)

THE / BOY EMIGRANTS. / by / Noah Brooks. / With Illustrations by Thomas Moran and / W. L. Sheppard. / New York: / Scribner, Armstrong and Company. / 1877.

Collation: yellow end paper; inserted fly leaf; fly leaf; half-title [p. i]; blank [p. ii]; inserted frontispiece; title page [p. iii]; copyright notice dated 1876 [p. iv]; dedication [pp. v–vi]; table of contents, pp. [vii]–viii; list of illustrations [p. ix]; blank [p. x]; text, pp. 1–309; blank [p. 310]; 12 pp. (6 leaves) publisher's advertisements, the last of which is for: *Popular and Standard Books . . . in 1875.;* fly leaf, inserted; yellow end paper.

Bound in several colors of cloth. The front cover is black-stamped: The / Boy Emigrants [*in cover color on black field*] / by / Noah Brooks [*in cover color on black field*] / There is also an arrangement of ornamental borders and rules. At the center is a circular vignette of an Indian and a boy at the rear of a covered wagon. The spine is lettered: The / Boy / Emigrants [*the three preceding lines in black on a gold field with floral design in cover color*] / by / Noah Brooks. [*the two preceding lines are in gold*] / [*gold vignette of the boy emigrants*] / Scribner, Armstrong / & Co [*publisher's imprint in gold*]   The spine is further decorated with rules in gold and black. The back cover is blind-stamped with front cover stamping.

All edges trimmed. Size of leaf, $7\frac{3}{8}'' \times 4\frac{7}{8}''$. Including the frontispiece there are twelve full-page plates, inserted. Other illustrations as listed at [p. ix] are textual.

All examined copies of the first edition, including two contemporary presentation copies, have a stub following [p. 310]

48

which is a conjugate of leaf constituting pp. 289–290. No definite reason for the excision has been advanced but it is quite possible that the page, a blank leaf(?), was removed by the publishers in order that the advertisements might be more prominently displayed.

Appeared serially in *St. Nicholas*, November 1875 to October 1876. Received at the Library of Congress November 16, 1876.

The first edition exists in two variant states as follows:

First: At the foot of the copyright page appears the following: John F. Trow & Son, / Printers, / 205–213 East 12th Street, / New York.

Second: Imprint at the same place reads: Trow's / Printing and Bookbinding Co., / 205–213 East 12th St., / New York. In this state the advertisements at the back of the book are not the same as those described in the collation above and carry blurbs for books published later than "The Boy Emigrants."

1880

HEZEKIAH BUTTERWORTH

(1839–1905)

ZIGZAG JOURNEYS / IN / EUROPE. / Vacation Rambles in Historic Lands. / by / Hezekiah Butterworth. / Boston: / Estes and Lauriat. / 1880.

Collation: end paper, printed in blue, black and yellow on white with a map of England and Scotland enclosed in decorative border; inserted fly-leaf; inserted frontispiece; title page [p. i]; copyright notice dated 1879 [p. ii]; preface, pp. [iii]–iv; table of contents [p. v]; blank [p. vi]; list of illustrations, pp. [vii]–viii; sub-title [p. 1]; illustration [p. 2]; text, pp. [3]–311; blank [p. 312]; inserted fly leaf; end paper: printed in blue, black and yellow on white with a map of France and Belgium.

Bound in cloth, red noted, but possibly issued in other colors. Covers stamped in black and gold. Front cover lettered: Zig-Zag Journeys [*gold, black and cover color*] / in [*black*] / Europe [*initial black and gold, otherwise gold*] / Vacation Rambles / in / Historic / Lands / [*last four lines in gold*] Further decorated in black and gold with vignette of "Father and the boys," equestrian statue, ornamental rules, border, etc. The spine is lettered: Zig-Zag / Journeys / [*2 preceding lines in black, on gold field*] / in / Europe / [*2 preceding lines in gold*] / [*the following in black:*] [*belfry-tower*] / Boston / Estes / & Lauriat [*spine further decorated with ornaments and rules in black*]

Issued in three bindings as indicated by Estes and Lauriat's advertisement in the *Publishers' Weekly,* August 23, 1879, where the publishers advertised copies in "illuminated board covers, $1.50; cloth, bevelled and gilt, $2.00; cloth, full gilt, $2.25." The board copies have the title and publisher's monogram on the front cover; large picture of the story's characters on the back cover.

HEZEKIAH BUTTERWORTH

All edges trimmed. Size of leaf, $8\frac{1}{4}'' \times 6\frac{1}{2}''$. All the illustrations, with the exception of the frontispiece, are integral parts of the book.

Received at the Library of Congress October 31, 1879.

1880

LUCRETIA PEABODY HALE

(1820–1900)

THE / PETERKIN PAPERS / by / Lucretia P. Hale / With Illustrations. / [*publisher's monogram*] / Boston: / James R. Osgood and Company, / 1880.

Collation: brown-coated on white end paper; inserted fly leaf; inserted frontispiece; title page [p. 1]; copyright notice [p. 2]; dedication [p. 3]; blank [p. 4]; preface, pp. [5]–10; table of contents [p. 11]; list of illustrations [p. 12]; text, pp. [13]–246; fly leaf; inserted fly leaf; end paper, as described.

Bound in twilled green cloth, black-stamped. The front cover is lettered: The / Peterkin / Papers / . Lucretia. P. Hale. / Decorated with a series of rules, arabesques, "stars," etc. The spine is gold-lettered except as noted: The / Peterkin / Papers / Lucretia P. Hale / Illustrated [*in black*] / James R. Osgood & Co.   Further stamped with a series of ornamental designs in gold and black.

All edges trimmed. Size of leaf, $7'' \times 4\frac{1}{2}''$. The illustrations as listed at [p. 12] are inserted and full page.

Appeared serially as early as 1868 in *Our Young Folks* and later, beginning in 1874, in *St. Nicholas*. Received at the Library of Congress November 18, 1880.

A continuation, later collected as "The Last of the Peterkins," *Boston*, 1886, appeared originally in *St. Nicholas*.

1880

THOMAS WALLACE KNOX

(1835–1896)

THE BOY TRAVELLERS IN THE FAR EAST /
[*rule*] / Adventures of / Two Youths in a Journey /
to / Japan and China / by / Thomas W. Knox /
Author of "Camp-Fire and Cotton-Field" "Overland
Through Asia" / "Underground" "John" etc. / Illustrated / [*publisher's seal*] / New York / Harper &
Brothers, Publishers / Franklin Square / 1880

Collation: end papers slate-grey on white, printed in black
with an all-over series of Oriental figures; inserted fly leaf
[pp. 1–2]; fly leaf [pp. 3–4]; colored frontispiece, inserted
[pp. 5–6]; title page [p. 7]; copyright notice dated 1879
[p. 8]; preface, pp. [9]–10; table of contents, pp. [11]–12;
list of illustrations, pp. [13]–16; text, pp. [17]–421; blank
[p. 422]; one leaf, publisher's advertisements; inserted fly
leaf; end paper, as described.

Bound in cloth, red noted, with stamping in gold, black
and silver. The front cover is gold-lettered: The / Boy Travellers. / Japan / and / China.   *Boy Travellers* is accented
with black. Top of the front cover is stamped with black and
gold decorations; lower portion of cover is stamped black,
gold and silver with cherry-branch and blossoms, pagoda, fish,
etc., and with *Thomas W. Knox.* in cover color on a black
field. The spine is gold-lettered: The / Boy / Travellers /
[*followed by, in cover color:*] [*dash*] / Knox. / [*followed
by, in gold:*] Japan / and / China   The spine is further decorated in gold, black and silver with coins, rat-line, etc. At
center of the back cover, in black and gold, is stamped an
ornamental fan incorporating the publisher's monogram.

All edges trimmed. Size of leaf $8\frac{13}{16}'' \times 6\frac{1}{2}''$. All illustrations, save the frontispiece, are integral parts of the book. Received for copyright at the Library of Congress November 29,
1879.

1880

HARRIET MULFORD STONE LOTHROP
(Margaret Sidney)
(1844–1924)

FIVE LITTLE PEPPERS / AND HOW THEY GREW / by / Margaret Sidney / [*decorative rule*] / Boston / D. Lothrop and Company / Franklin St. Corner of Hawley [1880]

Collation: yellow end paper; frontispiece; title page [p. 1]; copyright notice dated 1880 [p. 2]; dedication, p. 3; blank [p. 4]; table of contents, pp. 5–6; text, pp. 7–410; publisher's advertisements, 4 pp.; yellow end paper.

Noted in green, blue and brown cloths. Front cover and spine decorated with color-stamping, gilt and red tomato-like peppers. Front cover reads: Five / Little Peppers / and How They Grew / [*publisher's monogram*]   All lettering gold-stamped with the exception of the first two lines which are in color on gilt bands. In addition there are gold stamped figures of children. Spine reads: Five / Little / Peppers / and / How They Grew / [*gold-stamped figure of seated girl*] / D. Lothrop & Co.   First three lines in color on gilt bands, publisher's name in cover color, balance of lettering in gold.

In the first state of the first edition the copyright notice is dated 1880; later printings are dated either 1880 or 1881 but other bibliographical points are present and make identification of the first state possible. First state points: the caption for the illustration at p. 231 reads: . . . *said Polly.;* later: . . . *said Phronsie.* The advertisements at the back of the book have no mention of a contest; first state of the binding has the *&* in the publisher's monogram on the front cover gold-stamped; later: present in cover color and still later completely absent.

HARRIET MULFORD STONE LOTHROP

Soon after publication of the volume the firm became D. Lothrop Company, which fact is responsible for the disappearance of the ampersand. Naturally the first edition has the original form of the firm name on the copyright page; later printings D. Lothrop Company.

The copyright copy received at the Library of Congress, October 13, 1881, has all the required features of the first edition, the leaves measuring $7\frac{1}{16}'' \times 5''$.

In addition to the above collated states in cloth the publishers also issued at least two editions in colored pictorial boards with the sheets apparently printed from the magazine plates. Examination indicates beyond doubt that these were issued sometime after the first edition made its appearance.

1881

JOEL CHANDLER HARRIS

(1848–1908)

UNCLE REMUS / His Songs and His Sayings / The
Folk-Lore of the Old Plantation / [*picture of Uncle
Remus*] / by Joel Chandler Harris / With Illustrations
by Frederick S. Church and / James H. Moser / New
York / D. Appleton and Company / 1, 3, and 5 Bond
Street / 1881

Collation: butterfly-design printed end paper (various colors
noted) ; fly leaf; frontispiece; title page [p. 1]; copyright
notice dated 1880 [p. 2]; introduction, pp. [3]–12; table
of contents, pp. [13]–15; blank [p. 16]; sub-title [p. 17];
blank [p. 18]; text, pp. [19]–231; blank [p. 232]; publisher's advertisements, 8 pp., headed: *New Books;* fly leaf;
end paper, as described.

Bound in several colors of cloth. Front cover is black-
stamped with horizontal decorative rules at bottom; left of
cover is stamped with cane-stalk extending to top; double
black rules at top of cover. At right center, gold-stamped, is a
vignette of Br'er Rabbit smoking his pipe. Back cover is blind-
stamped with double-rule border. Spine is gold-stamped: [*decorative rule*] / Uncle / Remus / [*banjo*] His / Songs / &
His / Sayings / [*decorative rule*]

All edges trimmed. Size of leaf, 7½" scant × 5".

First appeared as a regular feature of the Atlanta *Constitu-
tion*, the first of the series appearing in 1879.

The following bibliographical note is taken directly from
Merle Johnson's "American First Editions," *New York,* 1936:
The advertisements at the back of the book do not contain any
mention or review of "Uncle Remus: His Songs and His Say-

ings." Mention of the title occurs in later printings. In the Julia Collier Harris book on Joel Chandler Harris there is a reproduction of an 1880 dated title page; Mrs. Harris states that the reproduction was made from a page that "was not an integral part of a book, but a loose leaf." It is probable that the page so reproduced was printed as either a proof or as a copyright measure. Thus far no copy with an 1880 title page has been recorded. Two copies of the first edition have been noted with the title page tipped-in on a stub; status unknown.

The Library of Congress records show no record of deposit date but a copyright entry covering the title was made March 27, 1880. It seems almost certain that this last was for the title page only since the *Publishers' Weekly* for September 11, 1880 and October 9, 1880 contain Appleton advertisements which state, respectively, "in press and in preparation" and "in press and nearly ready." The book was recorded as received in the *Publishers' Weekly*, December 4, 1880.

1881

EDWARD EVERETT HALE

(1822–1909)

(and) SUSAN HALE

(1833–1910)

A FAMILY FLIGHT / THROUGH / FRANCE, GERMANY, NORWAY AND / SWITZERLAND / by / Rev. E. E. Hale and Miss Susan Hale / Fully Illustrated / Boston / D. Lothrop & Company / Franklin Street [1881]

Collation: end paper printed light green with vine design; inserted fly leaf; frontispiece, recto blank [pp. 1–2]; title page [p. 3]; copyright notice dated 1881 [p. 4]; table of contents, pp. [5]–7; list of illustrations, pp. [8]–13; blank [p. 14]; text, pp. [15]–405; blank [p. 406]; end paper, as described.

Bound in green cloth stamped in red and gold. Front cover is red-lettered: A Family / Flight / France, / Germany, Norway, / Switzerland   At left center, in gold and red, is a vignette of birds, bags, walking-sticks, etc. On one of the bags, in red, is the name: Hale   The spine is red-lettered: A / Family / Flight / [*rule*] / Hale / [*banners and shield in red and gold*] / D. Lothrop & Co. / Boston   Edges of cover are bevelled.

All edges gilt. Size of leaf, $8\frac{11}{16}'' \times 6\frac{3}{8}''$. Illustrations as listed at pp. [8]–13 are integral parts of the book.

Received at the Library of Congress for copyright March 11, 1882.

1881

JAMES OTIS KALER
(James Otis)
(1848–1912)

TOBY TYLER / or / Ten Weeks With a Circus / by / James Otis / Illustrated / New York / Harper & Brothers, Franklin Square / 1881

Collation: end paper (*note:* these have been noted either coated with various colors; or, coated and printed with an all-over design. The file copy at the Library of Congress has the printed end papers but lacking other evidence it is impossible to state priority); fly leaf; frontispiece [pp. 1–2]; title page [p. 3]; copyright notice [p. 4]; table of contents [p. 5], blank [p. 6]; list of illustrations [p. 7]; blank [p. 8]; text, pp. [9]–265; blank [p. 266]; publisher's advertisements, pp. [1]–6; fly leaf; end paper, as described.

Bound in cloth, both orange and light brown noted. Front cover stamped: Toby Tyler [*in red, gilt and black*] / or [*in red and black*] / Ten Weeks With / a Circus [*both the preceding lines in red on a black band*]   Below the preceding is a circus coach and procession watched by small boy, stamped in red, black and gold. Spine is gold-lettered: Toby Tyler / or / Ten Weeks / With / a Circus [*on black field*] / [*red-stamped monkey in black-stamped cage*] / Harpers [*in red*]

The copy here collated, as with the file copy at the Library of Congress, has the spine stamping, with the exception of the publisher's name, placed at the center. Copies have been noted with the stamping about $\frac{3}{8}''$ from the top of spine. Thus far it has been impossible to establish priority for either state but significantly enough I have seen no copy of the reprint with the stamping at the top. All edges trimmed. Size of leaf, $6\frac{1}{4}'' \times 4\frac{13}{16}''$.

Received at the Library of Congress September 7, 1881.

1881

ROSSITER JOHNSON

(1840–1931)

PHAETON ROGERS / a Novel of Boy Life / by /
Rossiter Johnson / [*rule*] / Illustrated / [*rule*] / New
York / Charles Scribner's Sons / 743 and 745 Broad-
way / 1881

Collation: yellow end paper; frontispiece [pp. i–ii]; title
page [p. iii]; copyright notice [p. iv]; table of contents, pp.
[v]–vi; list of illustrations [p. vii]; blank [p. viii]; text, pp.
[1]–344; *Scribners' New List of Books for Young Folks,* 8
leaves (16 pp.); fly leaf; end paper, as described.

Bound in several colors of twilled cloth stamped with gold
and black. Front cover is stamped: Phaeton Rogers [*in gold*]
/ A Novel / of / Boy Life / [*"lightning-bolt" rule*] / Rossiter Johnson   Except as noted all stamping is in black.
Front cover is further decorated with a kite on the string of
which are three small shields one of which is lettered: *Look
Aloft*; printing press, Phaeton Rogers in fireman's helmet de-
scending flaming staircase. Spine is gold-lettered: Phaeton /
Rogers / [*rule*] / Johnson / Scribners   Spine is further
stamped, in black, with steeple to which is tied a string extending to the kite on the front cover.

All edges trimmed. Size of leaf, $7\frac{1}{8}''\times5\frac{1}{16}''$. All illustrations are printed as integral parts of the book.

Appeared serially in *St. Nicholas*, December, 1880, to October, 1881. Book published October 4, 1881.

1881

FRANK R. (FRANCIS RICHARD) STOCKTON

(1834–1902)

THE / FLOATING PRINCE / and other / Fairy Tales. / by / Frank R. Stockton. / New York: / Charles Scribner's Sons. / 1881.

Collation: end paper, green printed with illustrations from the text; inserted fly leaf; blank [p. 1]; frontispiece [p. 2]; title page [p. 3]; copyright notice [p. 4]; list of illustrations, pp. [5]–6; table of contents [p. 7]; blank [p. 8]; text, pp. 1-199; blank [p. 200]; 16 pp. (8 leaves) publisher's advertisements; inserted fly leaf; end paper, as described.

Bound in cloth, green and brown noted, gold and black stamped. The front cover is black-stamped: The / Floating / Prince / and / other / [*at right, in cover color on a black field, vertically arranged:*] Fairy . Tales . / [*at the lower left, in cover color on a black field:*] Frank . R Stockton   The front cover is further decorated with stamped scenes and characters from the text. The spine is stamped in black and gold: The / Floating / Prince / F. R. Stockton / and . other / Fairy Tales /   The spine is decorated with pictorial vignettes. Edges of the cover are bevelled.

All edges trimmed. Size of leaf, $8'' \times 6\frac{1}{2}''$. All illustrations are integral parts of the book.

The title story first appeared in *St. Nicholas,* December, 1880; the book was published November 1, 1881.

A copy in printed boards, title page dated 1884, is the earliest known copy to be so published. The publishers state that board-bound copies were not issued until September 23, 1884.

1882

DANIEL CARTER BEARD

(1850–   )

What to Do / and / How to / Do It / THE : AMER-
ICAN : BOYS / . HANDY : BOOK . / by / D. C.
Beard. / New-York / [*rule*] / Charles / Scribner's /
Sons. / 1882   Wholly enclosed by single-rule box
and with vignettes of boys engaged in ice-sailing, kiting,
etc.

Collation: yellow end paper; 2 fly leaves; title page [p. i];
copyright notice [p. ii]; preface, pp. [iii]–v; blank [p. vi];
table of contents, pp. [vii]–xiii; blank [p. xiv]; sub-title,
with vignette of fishing boy on verso [pp. 1–2]; text, pp.
[3]–382; index, pp. [383]–391; blank [p. 392]; *Scribner's
New List of Books for the Young 1882–1883* . . . , pp. [1]–
[16]; fly leaf; yellow end paper.

Bound in several colors of cloth stamped with gold and
black. The front cover is gold-stamped: The / American /
Boy's / Handy / Book   The front cover is further decorated with black stamping of boys engaged in various sports
and with facsimile autograph: *D. C. Beard* at lower right
corner. The spine is gold-lettered: The / American / Boy's
/ Handy / Book / [*facsimile autograph of the author*] /
Scribners   The spine is further decorated with black-
stamped vignettes of rope, boy archer, etc.

All edges trimmed. Size of leaf, $7\frac{5}{8}''\times5\frac{5}{8}''$.

Published October 4, 1882, in an edition of 3500 copies.

A companion volume, "How to Amuse Yourself and Others:
The American Girls Handy Book," by Lina and Adelia B.
Beard, was issued by the same publishers in 1887.

1882

JAMES BALDWIN

(1841–1925)

THE / STORY OF SIEGFRIED / by / James Baldwin / Illustrated by Howard Pyle / New York / Charles Scribner's Sons / 1882

Collation: green-coated on white end paper; fly leaf; inserted frontispiece; title page [p. i]; copyright notice [p. ii]; dedication [p. iii]; blank [p. iv]; foreword, pp. v–xiii; blank [p. xiv]; table of contents, pp. xv–xvi; list of illustrations [p. xvii]; blank [p. xviii]; sub-title [p. xix]; blank [p. xx]; text, pp. 1–290; Afterword, pp. 291–293; Notes, pp. 294–306; publisher's advertisements, 4 pp. (2 leaves); fly leaf; end paper, as described.

Issued in several colors of cloth stamped in gold and black. The front cover is lettered: The [*black*] / Story of [*gold*] / ∴ Siegfried [*gold*] /   To the left, on a vertical gold band and showing in cover color: Nothvng I am the Death that Bringeth Life O /   The cover is further stamped with an illustration after the frontispiece, "The Forging of Balmung," wholly black save for a gold-stamped "halo" background for the head and shoulders of Siegfried. The spine is gold lettered on a black field: The [*battle-ax in cover color*] / [*X decoration in cover color*] Story / of / Siegfried / [*at foot:*] Scribners   The spine is further stamped with conventional rule and box decorations in black; sword in cover color on a gold field; *I Am The Death That Bringeth Life* in black on a gold field; small serpent in cover color and black at point of the sword.

All edges trimmed. Size of leaf, $7\frac{3}{16}''\times 5\frac{3}{16}''$. The illustrations as listed at [p. xvii] are inserted.

Published October 4, 1882; received at the Library of Congress October 11, 1882.

1882

LOUISE-CLARKE PYRNELLE

DIDDIE, DUMPS, AND TOT / or / Plantation Child-Life / by / Louise-Clarke Pyrnelle / Illustrated / New York / Harper & Brothers, Franklin Square / 1882

Collation: end paper, printed in light green with an all-over floral design; 2 fly leaves, the first of which is inserted; frontispiece; title page [p. i]; copyright notice [p. ii]; dedication [p. iii]; blank [p. iv]; preface, pp. [v]–viii; table of contents [p. ix]; blank [p. x]; list of illustrations [p. xi]; blank [p. xii]; text, pp. [13]–217; blank [p. 218]; one leaf of publisher's advertisements; inserted fly leaf; end paper, as described.

Bound in light green twilled cloth with black stamping. Front cover stamped: Diddie Dumps & Tot [*in a broken line*] / or / Plantation Child-Life   Cover is decorated with a crescent moon, flying bats, stars, cotton-plant and ornamental border enclosing the title; at top center of the border is the publisher's monogram. Spine is stamped: [*cotton-plant branch*] / Diddie / Dumps / & / Tot / [*cotton-plant branch*] / The back cover is stamped with a flying bat, stars and cotton-plant branches. All cover decorations are so arranged that they present a unit when the covers are opened.

All edges trimmed. Size of leaf, $6\frac{1}{4}'' \times 4\frac{3}{4}''$.

Received for copyright at the Library of Congress October 14, 1882.

1882

SAMUEL LANGHORNE CLEMENS
(Mark Twain)

(1835–1910)

THE / PRINCE AND THE PAUPER / a Tale / For
Young People of all Ages / by / Mark Twain / With
One Hundred and Ninety-Two Illustrations / Boston
/ James R. Osgood and Company / 1882

Collation: end paper; fly leaf; blank [p. 1]; letter to Crom-
well in holograph facsimile [p. 2]; transcript of the preceding [p. 3]; the great seal [p. 4]; title page [p. 5]; copyright
notice dated 1881 [p. 6]; dedication [p. 7]; blank [p. 8];
quotation from *The Merchant of Venice* [p. 9]; blank [p.
10]; table of contents, pp. 11–12; list of illustrations, pp.
13–18; author's note [p. 19]; blank [p. 20]; sub-title [p.
21]; blank [p. 22]; text, pp. 23–401; blank [p. 402]; sub-
title [p. 403]; blank [p. 404]; notes, pp. 405–411; blank
[p. 412]; 2 fly leaves; end paper.

Issued in green cloth and various leathers. Cloth copies are
stamped as follows on the front cover; in gold: The Prince /
and / The Pauper / Mark Twain / [*in black: suns, shields,
etc. At the upper left is gold-stamped a crown, shield, scepter,
globe, etc.*]   The spine is gold-stamped: The / Prince / and
the / Pauper / Mark Twain / James R. Osgood / & Co.
The spine is further decorated with black-stamped ornaments.
The first four lines are cover color on a gold field.

The first state of the first edition carries the imprint of the
Franklin Press on the copyright page.

All edges trimmed. Size of leaf, 8¼″ full × 6½″ full.

Copies received at the Library of Congress December 12,
1881, although copyright had been granted October 13, 1881.

The London edition, published by Chatto and Windus, was issued on December 1, 1881, and apparently was published weeks before the American edition.

In addition to the trade edition as collated above the publishers issued a small number of copies in white cloth, printed on China paper. In two known copies presented by the author to friends he wrote that the edition was limited to six copies. This number is probably incorrect inasmuch as the copy presented by a member of the Osgood firm carries an inscription stating that the edition was limited to fourteen copies. However, six or fourteen, the book is a genuine rarity in the China paper state.

No previous magazine or periodical publication. A chapter, "A Boy's Adventure," otherwise known as "The Whipping Boy's Story," appeared in *The Bazaar Budget*, June 4, 1880. Intended as part of the novel the author decided not to include it. The chapter was privately printed as a four page leaflet *circa* 1929, in a single sheet folded once to make four pages.

1883

GEORGE WILBUR PECK

(1840–1916)

PECK'S / BAD BOY / AND HIS PA. / by Geo. W. Peck, / Author of "Peck's Fun," "Peck's Sunshine," and Editor "Peck's Sun." / With Illustrations by Gean Smith. / [*rule*] / Chicago: / Belford, Clarke & Co. / 1883.

Collation: issued in several colors of cloth and printed paper wrappers. The copy here collated is bound in brown cloth. Decorated end paper; frontispiece [pp. i–ii]; title page [p. iii]; copyright notice [p. iv]; *A Card From the Author* [p. v]; blank [p. vi]; table of contents, pp. [vii]–xiv; list of illustrations [p. xv]; blank [p. xvi]; text, pp. [9]–196; 14 pp. publisher's advertisements preceded by divisional sub-title page; decorated end paper.

The front cover is stamped with a picture of the side of a house lettered: Pecks / Bad / Boy   To the left of the lettering Pa is portrayed hanging from a window-sill, his legs on either side of: and / his / Pa   The spine is gold-stamped: [*decorative rule*] / Pecks / [*decoration*] / Bad / Boy / and His / Pa / [*five small circles arranged cross-wise*] / [*sun decoration*] / [*decorative rule*]

All edges trimmed. Size of leaf, $7\frac{1}{8}'' \times 4\frac{3}{4}''$.

The first state of the first edition may be bound in either cloth or printed wrappers but must have no text, save the advertisements, after p. 196; later printings of the book have added text following this page. The earliest state of the copyright page has the rules above and below the copyright notice at [p. iv] a full $\frac{7}{8}$ of an inch apart; later printings either lack the rules or have them spaced differently. A copy bound in flexible leather, asserted to be and quite possibly, the author's

GEORGE WILBUR PECK

personal copy, has the rules on the copyright page as here described. There are certain other variations of the copyright
page but the most certain identification lies in the rules. For
years both collectors and dealers have claimed priority for
those copies having unbroken type at the last line of p. 196.
There can be no argument that the first printed copies have
the type unbroken but it cannot be claimed that all copies of
the first printing have the type in perfect state. Copies in
wrappers have interior of grocery store printed on front cover.
It would appear that the printers ran short on the capital letter *B*, substituting the letter *R* in several of the running heads,
changing the reading to *Roy*. This persists through several of
the early printings and is therefore of no value in first state
determination.

Received at the Library of Congress March 1, 1883.

The earliest copies do not have in the front matter "A Card from the
Author" dated *Milwaukee, Feb., 1883*. Copies without this feature are
so seldom found that one may be permitted the suspicion that they
represent a pre-publication issue.

68

1883

(ELIZABETH) LIZZIE WILLIAMS CHAMPNEY

(1850–1922)

THREE / VASSAR GIRLS / ABROAD. / Rambles of Three College Girls on a Vacation Trip / Through France and Spain for Amusement / and Instruction. / With Their Haps and Mishaps. / by / Lizzie W. Champney, / Author of "A Neglected Corner of Europe," etc. / With Nearly a Hundred and Fifty Original Illustrations by "Champ" / (J. Wells Champney) and other Distinguished Artists. / [*decorative rule*] / Boston: / Estes and Lauriat. / 1883.

Collation: light-buff on white end paper, printed yellow and black with map of France, Spain, Northern Africa, etc.; fly leaf [pp. i–ii]; blank [p. iii]; frontispiece [p. iv]; title page [p. v]; copyright notice dated 1882 [p. vi]; table of contents [p. vii]; blank [p. viii]; list of illustrations, pp. [ix]–x; sub-title [p. xi]; blank [pp. xii–xiii]; full-page illustration [p. xiv]; text, pp. [15]–236; 2 blank fly leaves; end paper, as described.

Bound in brown cloth stamped in black and gold. The front cover is gold-stamped: Vassar / Girls [*the two preceding lines at center of cover*] / Three [*to left of preceding*] / Abroad [*to right of central lettering* / [*below preceding, also in gold, is stamped vignette of the three girls.*] Further decorated with black and gold-stamped Moorish arches, mosaic floor, pillars, etc. At bottom of cover, in black: . Estes & Lauriat . The spine is gold-lettered: Three / Vassar / Girls /Abroad / [*the following in black:*] . By . / . Lizzie . / . W . / . Champney . / [*gold-stamped vignette of girl*] / [*the two lines following in black:*] . Boston . / . Estes and

(ELIZABETH) LIZZIE WILLIAMS CHAMPNEY

Lauriat .   At top and bottom is a black-stamped decorative rule; triple-rule in black above and below publisher's name.

All edges trimmed. Size of leaf, $8\frac{3}{16}''\times 6\frac{5}{8}''$.

Also issued in illuminated boards with similar decorations. In the board state the back cover is wholly printed with an arabesque design. Collation the same as cloth-bound copies save that copies in cloth are $\frac{1}{8}''$ narrower in the page.

Received at the Library of Congress September 21, 1882.

1883

EDWARD EGGLESTON

(1837–1902)

THE HOOSIER / SCHOOL-BOY / by / Edward
Eggleston / Illustrated / New York / Charles Scribner's Sons / 1883

Collation: brown-coated on white end paper; inserted fly
leaf; half-title [p. i]; blank [p. ii]; blank (recto frontispiece)
[p. iii]; frontispiece, *"Cousin Sukey," said* . . . [p. iv]; title
page [p. v]; copyright notice [p. vi]; table of contents, pp.
[vii]–ix; blank [p. x]; list of illustrations [p. xi]; blank [p.
xii]; text, pp. [9]–181; blank [p. 182]; 4 leaves (8 pp.)
publisher's advertisements; fly leaf; end paper, as described.
The first page of advertisements is inserted on a stub compris-
ing a portion of leaf pp. 175–176. No reason for this can-
cellation has been determined nor has any examined copy of
this state been found to contain the leaf as an integral part of
the signature.

Bound in several colors of cloth. From the variety of colors
used in the cover stamping it appears that the binder was
allowed to use his own judgment. No attempt to describe the
colors used is given here. The front cover is lettered: The
Hoosier / School-Boy: / [*vignette of the Boy*] / by / Edwar^d
Eggleston: The spine is lettered: The / Hoosier / School
/ Boy: / [*vignette: books and carrying strap*] / by / Edwar^d /
Eggleston / Scribners

All edges trimmed. Size of leaf, $7\frac{1}{4}''$ scant $\times$ $5\frac{3}{16}''$.

A copy with the frontispiece as described above was received
at the Library of Congress October 1, 1883. Appeared serially
in *St. Nicholas* December, 1881, to April, 1882.

The above collation is of the earliest known state of the
first edition. It is to be noted that the pagination is faulty and

that the first page of text is numbered [9] although properly it should be [13]. In the later issues the frontispiece is that of the Hoosier school-room interior and depicts "Old Ball," switch in hand, listening to young Christopher Columbus reciting "The Better Land." In the first state the illustrations are placed as follows:

"Cousin Sukey," . . . frontispiece, [pp. iii–iv]. An integral part of the book.
"Not There . . ." [pp. 33–34]. Inserted.
Jack Amusing . . . [pp. 37–38]. Inserted.
"The Landing . . ." [pp. 113–114]. Inserted.
Bob Holliday . . . [pp. 179–180]. Inserted.

The illustrations are listed in the above order at [p. xi]. In the later states the illustrations are placed as follows:

"Not There . . ." frontispiece, [pp. iii–iv]. An integral part of the book.
Jack Amusing . . . [pp. 37–38]. Inserted.
"Cousin Sukey," . . . inserted between pp. [86]–87 but is not reckoned in the pagination.
"The Landing . . ." [pp. 113–114]. Inserted.
Bob Holliday . . . [pp. 179–180]. Inserted.

For the further identification of the first state here follows the collation of the first pages of the text.

Chapter 1: pp. [9]–16
Chapter 2: pp. [17]–21
Chapter 3: pp. [22]–28
Chapter 4: pp. [29]–30–31–32–[inserted and considered as pp. 33–34 is the illustration, *"Not There . . ."*]–35.

Collation of the first four chapters in *State B*:

Chapter 1: pp. [11]–18
Chapter 2: pp. [19]–23
Chapter 3: pp. [24]–30
Chapter 4: pp. [31]–35

The finished books were delivered to the publishers September 19, 1883, and published September 22, 1883. Of the first edition 105 copies were supplied the New York publishing house of Orange, Judd with their imprint.

1883

HOWARD PYLE

(1853–1911)

THE / MERRY ADVENTURES [*in red*] / OF / ROBIN HOOD / OF GREAT RENOWN, IN NOT-TINGHAMSHIRE. / Written and Illustrated / by Howard Pyle. [*in red*] / [*rule*] / [*monograms of author and publisher, combined*] / [*double rule*] / New York: [*in red*] / Printed by Charles Scribner's Sons at [*decoration*] / No. 743 & 745 Broadway, and Sold by Same / [*rule*] / MDCCCLXXXIII. [*in red*] [1883] Lettered by hand and with the artist-author's monogram at the lower right corner. Entirely enclosed by hand-drawn border.

Collation: brown-coated on white end paper; 2 fly leaves; half-title [p. i]; blank [p. ii]; frontispiece [pp. iii–iv]; title page [p. v]; copyright notice [p. vi]; preface, pp. [vii]–viii; table of contents, pp. [ix]–xvi; list of illustrations, pp. [xvii]–xx; picture of Robin Hood and the tall stranger printed on verso of leaf [pp. xxi–xxii], recto blank; text, pp. 1–296; fly leaf; end paper, as described.

Bound in full leather with the sides wholly blind-stamped with an all-over design. At the center is: [*ornament*] The. / Merry. / Adventures. / of / Robin.Hood. / Howard.Pyle. / Honi.Soit.Qui.Mal.Y.Pense. / [*publisher's monogram*] The spine is totally blind-stamped with an all-over decoration and with a leather label stamped in gold reading: Adventures. of. / Robin-Hood / [*rule*] / Pyle. Double-rules in gold at top and bottom of label. At foot of spine, blind-stamped: 1883

All edges trimmed and red-stained. Size of leaf, $9\frac{7}{16}''$ × $7\frac{1}{4}''$. Copies have been noted with slightly varying measurements.

HOWARD PYLE

Published October 23, 1883, in an edition of 3000 copies. Of this number 510 copies were sent in sheets to Sampson, Low & Company of London for English distribution.

1885

SAMUEL LANGHORNE CLEMENS
(Mark Twain)

(1835–1910)

ADVENTURES / OF / HUCKLEBERRY FINN /
(Tom Sawyer's Comrade). / Scene: The Mississippi
Valley. / Time: Forty to Fifty Years Ago. / by / Mark
Twain. / With One Hundred and Seventy-four Illustra-
tions. / New York: / Charles L. Webster and Com-
pany. / 1885.

Collation: light-peach tinted end paper; fly leaf; half title
[p. 1]; frontispiece [p. 2], portrait of Mark Twain, inserted;
title page [p. 3]; copyright notice dated 1884 [p. 4]; *Notice*
[p. 5]; blank [p. 6]; *Explanatory* [p. 7]; blank [p. 8]; table
of contents, pp. [9]–12; list of illustrations, pp. [13]–15;
blank [p. 16]; text, pp. [17]–366; 2 fly leaves, one of which
is inserted; end paper, as described. Not all copies have the
inserted fly leaf at the back.

Issued in several types of leather and in blue and green
cloths. No known priority for any of the various bindings
which were, in all likelihood, issued simultaneously as indicated by a letter written by Mark Twain to his publishers.
Cloth copies are stamped on the front cover: Adventures / of
/ Huckleberry / Finn. / (Tom Sawyer's Comrade.) / by /
Mark Twain. / [*ornamental branch*] / Illustrated.   At the
center-left is a vignette of Huck stamped in black and cover
color with a background of fence; the latter is gold-stamped.
Wholly enclosed by double-rule box. All stamping in black
except as noted and the lettering as italicized which is in gold.
The spine is stamped: [*double rule*] / [*row of dots*] / [*rule*]
/ Adventures / of / Huckleberry / [*ornament*] Finn. / [*rule*]
/ [*ornamental branch*] / by / Mark Twain. / Charles. L.
Webster / & Co. / [*double-rule*]   The spine stamping is

SAMUEL LANGHORNE CLEMENS

in black save for the title background, *by / Mark Twain.* and the publisher's name which are gold-stamped.

All edges trimmed. Size of leaf, $8\frac{7}{16}''\times 6\frac{5}{8}''$. This measurement is usual; copies have been noted that vary slightly.

The English edition was published December 4, 1884, a few days before the American edition was received at the Library of Congress for copyright.

This book remains one of the most perplexing of all bibliographical problems. An exhaustive discussion appears at pp. 43–50, Merle Johnson's "A Bibliography of Mark Twain," *New York,* 1935. From the mass of conjecture and supposition that surrounds this book the following definite points emerge:

p. 57, line 23, must read *was* for *saw*

Him and Another Man must be listed at [p. 13] as appearing at p. 88; later changed to p. 87.

The second 5 in the folio *155* appears in several states or entirely lacking. Nothing definite on this point has been established but it is certain that in late printings the second five is larger than the first and extends below the line of the first.

P. 283 may be present as an integral part of the signature or on a stub. It is obvious that very late copies have the page as an integral part of the signature; equally obvious that if the blemish that caused alteration of the page occurred after copies had been printed, the very first copies would also have the page an integral part of the signature.

The Mark Twain portrait frontispiece occurs in numerous states but it is generally agreed that the first states bear the imprint of the Heliotype Printing Co.

Adding to the puzzle is the fact that the Huck Finn frontispiece and the title page often occur in tipped-in state. Nothing definite on this feature has been established.

At p. 161 the signature number is lacking. Continued search has resulted in discovery of but one copy with the number present . . . but the copy bore the Canadian imprint and the number had every appearance of having been reset, but I have seen no copy of the American edition of any year with the signature number present. Discovery of an American copy with that signature number will be of the utmost bibliographical importance.

———————————

Basically the above description is correct but further study has greatly clarified the problem. See "In Re *Huckleberry Finn,*" by Jacob Blanck, in *The New Colophon,* N. Y., 1950, for a fuller discussion.

1886

CHARLES EDWARD CARRYL

(1842–1920)

DAVY AND THE GOBLIN / or / What Followed
Reading "Alice's Adventures / in Wonderland" / by /
Charles E. Carryl / Illustrated / [*publisher's seal*] /
Boston / Ticknor and Company / 1886

Collation: end paper, printed with an all-over design; fly
leaf; blank [p. 1]; frontispiece [p. 2]; title page [p. 3];
copyright notice dated 1885 [p. 4]; dedication [p. 5]; blank
[p. 6]; table of contents, pp. [7]–8; list of illustrations, pp.
[9]–10; text, pp. [11]–160; illustration [p. 161]; blank [p.
162]; publisher's advertisements, *Some Interesting Books*
. . . , numbered [i]–xiv [pp. 163–176]; inserted fly leaf;
end paper, as described.

Bound in several colors of cloth with the stamping in gold
and brown or gold and black; possibly other color combina-
tions. The front cover is gold-lettered on brown (or black)
ribbon: Davy $\overset{\text{and}}{\text{the}}$ Goblin / Illustrated / Charles E. Carryl
Stamped in brown or black are decorations of mice, Goblin,
Davy at the fire-place, etc. Spine is gold-lettered: Davy / and
⊙ / ⊙ the / Goblin / Illustrated / Carryl / Ticknor & Co.
Further stamped in brown or black with rules, ornaments,
Goblin, etc.

All edges trimmed and stained in several shades of yellow
or orange. Size of leaf, $8\frac{5}{16}'' \times 6\frac{1}{2}''$. The end papers have
been noted in various colors.

Appeared serially in *St. Nicholas*, December 1884 to March
1885. Received for copyright at the Library of Congress October 26, 1885.

The first edition exists in two states. At p. xi of the publisher's advertisements at the back of the book the following differences occur:

First State		*Second State*
	Line 20	
". . . Corea . . ."		". . . Korea . . ."
	Line 23	
". . . Coreans . . ."		". . . Koreans . . ."
	Line 26	
". . . Corean . . ."		". . . Korean . . ."
	Line 30	
". . . Coreans' . . ."		". . . Koreans' . . ."

In both first and second states the K spelling is given at p. xii of the advertisements.

1886

JANE ANDREWS

(1835–1887)

TEN BOYS / WHO LIVED ON / THE ROAD
FROM LONG AGO / TO NOW / by / Jane Andrews / Author of "Seven Little Sisters," "Geograph-
ical / Plays of United States," Etc. / Boston / Lee and
Shepard Publishers / New York Charles T. Dillingham / 1886

Collation: yellow end paper; fly leaf; inserted frontispiece;
title page, copyright notice dated 1885 on verso; dedication,
list of Andrews' works on verso; preface [pp. 1–2]; table
of contents, p. 3; blank [p. 4]; text, pp. 5–240; illustration
on coated paper, inserted; fly leaf; yellow end paper.

Bound in twilled yellow cloth with the front cover black-
stamped: Ten Boys / Who Lived on the Road / from /
Long Ago to Now   The front cover is further stamped
with vignettes of a Puritan, helmet, Horatius' sword, etc. The
spine, in cover color on a gold field, is stamped: Ten Boys /
Who / Lived on the Road / From / Long Ago / To Now
The spine is decorated with black-stamped sun, railroad loco-
motive, rules, shield, etc. At the foot of the spine is stamped:
Lee and Shepard

All edges trimmed. Size of leaf, $6\frac{3}{4}''$ scant $\times$ $4\frac{7}{8}''$.

In addition to the frontispiece and the illustration following the last page of text there are inserted also eight full page
plates on coated paper.

Received for copyright at the Library of Congress November
9, 1885.

1886

FRANCES HODGSON BURNETT

(1849–1924)

LITTLE LORD FAUNTLEROY / by / Frances Hodgson Burnett / [*vignette of servants and the sleeping Lord Fauntleroy*] / New-York / Charles Scribner's Sons / 1886

Collation: brown-coated on white end paper; fly leaf; blank [pp. i–ii]; half-title [p. iii]; blank [p. iv]; frontispiece [pp. v–vi]; title page [p. vii]; copyright notice [p. viii]; list of illustrations, pp. ix–xi; blank [p. xii]; text, pp. [1]–209; seal of the De Vinne Press [p. 210]; publisher's advertisements, 14 pp.; fly leaf; end paper, as described.

Bound in cloth, several shades of brown and slate blue noted, with end papers to match. The front cover is stamped in red, black and gold as follows: Little / Lord / Fauntleroy [*preceding three lines in black on a red ribbon*] / Frances Hodgson Burnett [*in red, initial letters accented with black*] Cover is further decorated with lions, crowns in red, black and red and black in combination; lower right is sketch of little girl at writing table; left center, on field of red touched with black, gilt-stamped vignette of the little lord with dog. The spine is stamped: Little / Lord / Fauntleroy / Frances Hodgson / Burnett / Scribners   The title is gold-stamped, accented with black; names of author and publisher in red. Further decorated with lions, crowns, dots in gilt, red and black.

All edges trimmed. Size of leaf, $8\frac{5}{16}$" $\times$ $6\frac{5}{8}$".

Appeared serially in *St. Nicholas*, November 1885 to October 1886. Published October 7, 1886 in an edition of 10,000 copies printed by the De Vinne Press and with their insignia at [p. 210]. Later editions were printed by J. J. Little whose first delivery of copies was on October 26, 1886.

FRANCES HODGSON BURNETT

A copy dated 1886 has been noted with no printer's imprint but since the book contains advertisements of books issued after first publication of "Little Lord Fauntleroy" it is obvious that such copies are of a late printing.

1886

AMELIA EDITH (HUDDLESTON) BARR

(1831–1919)

THE / BOW OF ORANGE RIBBON / A Romance
of New York / by / Amelia E. Barr / Author of "Jan
Vedder's Wife," "A Daughter of / Fife," etc. / [*rule*]
/ New York / Dodd, Mead and Company / 1886

Collation: yellow end paper; inserted fly leaf; title page
[p. i]; copyright notice [p. ii]; dedication [p. iii]; blank
[p. iv]; table of contents [p. v]; blank [p. vi]; text, pp.
1–444; postscript, p. 445; blank [p. 446]; yellow end paper.
Page 443–[446] constitute a single signature and are inserted.

Bound in twilled greenish-grey cloth with gold stamping.
The front cover is lettered: The Bow of Orange Ribbon /
[*rule*] / Amelia E. Barr / "All. These. Inconveniences. are.
Incident. / To. Love—Reproaches. Jealousies. Quarrels. /
Reconcilements. War. and. then. Peace.   The spine is let-
tered: The Bow / of / Orange / Ribbon / . Barr . / Dodd,
Mead ·· / & Company

All edges trimmed. Size of leaf, $6\frac{3}{4}''$ full $\times$ $4\frac{5}{8}''$.

Received at the *Publishers' Weekly* and recorded in the issue
of November 13, 1886. Received at the Library of Congress
October 20, 1886.

1887

KIRK MUNROE

(1850–1930)

THE FLAMINGO FEATHER / by / Kirk Munroe / Author of "Wakulla" etc. / Illustrated / New York / Harper & Brothers, Franklin Square / 1887

Collation: end paper, printed with all-over design; fly leaf; frontispiece; title page [p. i]; copyright notice with list of books in the *Harper's Young Folks Series* [p. ii]; table of contents [p. iii]; blank [p. iv]; list of illustrations, pp. [v]–vi; text, pp. [1]–255; blank [p. 256]; fly leaf; end paper, as described.

Bound in dark maroon cloth, front cover decorated with stamped flamingo feather in red and gold. Lettered in gold: The / Flamingo / Feather   Spine gold-lettered: The / Flamingo / Feather / Munroe / [*red flamingo wading in gold-stamped pool*] / Harpers

All edges trimmed. Size of leaf $6\frac{5}{16}''\times4\frac{13}{16}''$.

Received for copyright at the Library of Congress April 30, 1887.

1887

PALMER COX

(1840–1924)

THE BROWNIES: / Their Book / by / Palmer Cox
/ [*publisher's ornament*] / Published by / The Century Co. / New-York [1887]

Collation: buff-coated on white end paper; fly leaf [pp.
i–ii]; printed bookplate, p. iii; blank [p. iv]; title page [p.
v]; copyright notice, p. vi; explanatory note, p. vii; blank
[p. viii]; table of contents, pp. ix–xi; blank [p. xii]; text,
pp. 1–144; fly leaf; end paper, as described.

Bound in light green glazed boards. Front cover lettered
in brown: The / Brownies / Their Book   Below this is an
orange box within which is, orange-lettered with brown outline: By / Palmer / [*brown decoration*] Cox [*brown decoration*]   The cover is ornamented with Brownies printed in
orange, blue and brown. At the center of the back cover,
printed in brown and orange, is the publisher's ornament; at
the lower left corner, a few Brownies printed in color are
depicted running off the cover. The spine is lettered, reading
sideways: The Brownies / Their Book   At the top and the
foot of the spine is the publisher's ornament and at the bottom: The Century Co. The spine is further imprinted with
Brownies climbing a ladder.

All edges trimmed. Size of leaf, $9\frac{5}{8}'' \times 8\frac{1}{16}''$.

The first state of the first edition has the De Vinne Press
seal immediately below the copyright notice; later states have
the seal about two and one half inches from the bottom of the
page.

Appeared first, over a period of time, in various numbers
of *St. Nicholas*. Received at the Library of Congress September 27, 1887.

1887

JAMES BALDWIN

(1841–1925)

A STORY / OF / THE GOLDEN AGE / by / James Baldwin / Author of "The Story of Siegfried," etc. / Illustrated by Howard Pyle / New York / Charles Scribner's Sons / 1887

Collation: green-coated on white end paper; blank [p. i]; list of books "by the same author" [p. ii]; inserted frontispiece; title page [p. iii]; copyright notice [p. iv]; dedication [p. v]; blank [p. vi]; foreword, pp. vii–ix; blank [p. x]; table of contents, pp. xi–xii; sub-title [p. xiii]; blank [p. xiv]; list of illustrations, inserted [p. xv] (immediately below is a list of two maps); blank [p. xvi]; text, pp. 1–267; blank [p. 268]; afterword, pp. 269–272; notes, pp. 273–277; blank [p. 278]; inserted folding map; index to proper names, pp. 279–286; 8 pages publisher's advertisements; inserted fly leaf; end paper, as described.

Bound in several colors of cloth stamped with grey, white, black, silver and gold. The front cover is gold lettered: A Story of the / Golden Age   Below this, and extending to the bottom of the cover, stamped in the above colors, is a picture of Apollo slaying the python. The spine is stamped: [*row of black-stamped dots*] / A Story / of the / Golden / Age [*the preceding four lines in gold on a black field*] / Baldwin [*in gold on silver background embodying vignette of Thetis rising from the waves*] / Scribners. [*in gold*]

All edges trimmed. Size of leaf $7\frac{1}{4}'' \times 5\frac{1}{4}''$ scant. Illustrations as listed at [p. xv] are inserted; the two maps listed at the same page are also inserted.

Received at the Library of Congress October 27, 1887; published October 26, 1887 in an edition of 2,650 copies of which 500 were sent in sheets to Sampson, Low & Company, London.

1887

KATE DOUGLAS (SMITH) WIGGIN

(1856–1923)

THE BIRDS' CHRISTMAS CAROL / by / Kate
Douglas Wiggin / C. A. Murdock & Co. / 532 Clay
Street, San Francisco / 1887

Collation: end paper; half title [p. 1]; blank [p. 2]; title
page [p. 3]; copyright notice dated 1886 [p. 4]; dedication
[p. 5]; 4 lines of poetry [p. 6]; table of contents [p. 7];
blank [p. 8]; text, pp. [9]–67; blank [p. 68]; end paper.

Bound in cream colored wrappers. Front cover printed in
red: The Birds' / Christmas / Carol [*holly leaf*] / Kate .
Douglas . Wiggin .   Above the lettering, also in red, is a
ribbon decoration on which is a staff of music, holly-branch
and bird. Issued in a dust-wrapper of drab butcher paper with
the printing of the front wrapper repeated in black. The
wrapper has been noted in two colors but there is no apparent
priority.

All edges trimmed. Size of leaf, $6\frac{3}{16}''\times5\frac{7}{8}''$.

Received at the Library of Congress December 31, 1886.

1888

ROBERT GRANT

(1852–   )

JACK HALL / or / The School Days of an American / Boy / by / Robert Grant / Author of "Face to Face," "The Confessions of a Frivolous Girl," / etc. / Illustrated by F. G. Attwood / Boston / Jordan, Marsh and Company / 1888

Collation: Manila-yellow end paper; fly leaf; frontispiece; title page [p. i]; copyright notice dated 1887 [p. ii]; dedication [p. iii]; blank [p. iv]; table of contents, pp. [v]–vi; text, pp. [1]–394; fly leaf; end paper, as described.

Noted in both blue and brown cloths. Front cover is gilt-lettered, on a black field: Jack / Hall / or the / School Days / of an / American / Boy / Robert Grant   Further decorated with vignettes stamped in black. The back cover has a black-stamped vignette of an oarsman in a scull. Spine gold-lettered on a black field: Jack Hall / or the / School / Days / of an / American / Boy / [*rule*] / Grant / [*rule*]   Spine further decorated with black-stamped "escape by rope-ladder" vignette and, in black, at the foot of spine: Jordan, Marsh / & Co.

All edges trimmed. Size of leaf, $7\frac{3}{8}'' \times 4\frac{7}{8}''$.

Received at the Library of Congress for copyright October 8, 1887.

1888

FRANCES HODGSON BURNETT

(1849–1924)

EDITHA'S BURGLAR / A Story for Children / by / Frances Hodgson Burnett / Illustrated by / Henry Sandham. / Boston / Jordan, Marsh & Company / 1888

Collation: end paper; frontispiece [pp. 1–2]; title page [p. 3]; copyright notice [p. 4]; blank [p. 5]; in facsimile autograph, a letter from Elsie Leslie Lyde [pp. 6–7]; blank [p. 8]; list of illustrations [p. 9]; blank [p. 10]; text, pp. [11]– 64; end paper, [p. 2] imprinted with publisher's advertisements.

Bound in several colors of cloth. The front cover is stamped in black and gold: Editha's [*on decorative ribbon*] / [*silhouette of Editha in cover color surrounded by golden halo-effect; both on black field*] / Burglar [*on decorative ribbon*] / Frances Hodgson Burnett / [*shield and leaf ornament enclosing illustrator's initials:* H S] / wholly enclosed by single-rule box. All black-stamped save the halo.

In the first state of the first edition the frontispiece is that of Editha (as played by Elsie Leslie Lyde) posed at side of a chair in a crouching position; later states have a picture of Editha-Elsie seated. The first state is also distinguished by the presence of the Rand Avery imprint on the copyright page.

All edges trimmed. Size of leaf, $7\frac{3}{16}''\times5\frac{13}{16}''$.

First appeared in *St. Nicholas*, February 1880. Received for copyright at the Library of Congress July 11, 1888.

1888

THOMAS NELSON PAGE

(1853–1922)

TWO LITTLE CONFEDERATES / by / Thomas Nelson Page / Illustrated / New York / Charles Scribner's Sons / 1888

Collation: yellow end paper; fly leaf; half title, with advertisements for "In Ole Virginia" and "Befo' de War" on the verso; frontispiece; title page, copyright notice on verso; dedication, verso blank; list of illustrations, verso blank; text, pp. 1–156; publisher's advertisements, 10 pp.; fly leaf; yellow end paper.

Bound in light blue cloth stamped with dark blue, white and gold. Front cover is stamped: Two / Little / Confederates [*the three lines preceding in gold*] / [*picture in black and white after the illustration at p. 131*] / by / Thomas Nelson Page [*the two lines preceding in dark blue*] [*decoration in dark blue and white*]   The *T* in *Two* is accented in white and dark blue and extends the depth of the first three lines.

The spine is gold-lettered: [*decoration in dark blue and white*] / Two / Little / Confederates / [*decoration in dark blue, white and gold*] / by / Thomas / Nelson / Page / [*rules in dark blue, white and gold*] / Illustrated / [*canteen and strap in dark blue and white*] / Scribners

All edges trimmed. Size of leaf, $8\frac{1}{4}'' \times 6\frac{5}{8}''$.

Appeared serially in *St. Nicholas*, May to October, 1888. Published in book form in an edition of 2,835 copies, October 10, 1888.

1888

FRANCES COURTENAY BAYLOR
(BARNUM)

(1848–1920)

JUAN AND JUANITA / by / Frances Courtenay Baylor / Author of "On Both Sides," "Behind the Blue / Ridge," etc. / With Illustrations by Henry Sandham / [*publisher's monogram*] / Boston / Ticknor and Company / 1888

Collation: end paper, printed gold-brown on white with an all-over floral design; fly leaf; frontispiece; title page [p. 1]; copyright notice dated 1887 [p. 2]; dedication [p. 3]; blank [p. 4]; preface [p. 5]; blank [p. 6]; table of contents, pp. [7]–8; list of illustrations, pp. [9]–10; text, pp. [11]–276; fly leaf, inserted; end paper, as described.

Bound in olive-green cloth with gold and dark brown stamping. Front cover gold lettered: Juan and Juanita / Frances Courtenay Baylor / [*star-like ornament*] / Illustrated   The following dark brown: pictures of Juan and Juanita, dog, goats, birds, etc., the whole enclosed by double rule box. The spine is stamped: [*Double rule*] / Juan / and / Juanita / [*scroll*] / Baylor / Illustrated / [*triple rule*] / [*bow and arrow-filled quiver*] / [*triple rule*] / Ticknor / & Co. / [*double rule*]   All lettering and scroll under title in gold; balance in brown.

All edges trimmed and stained red. Size of leaf, $8\frac{5}{16}''$ × $6\frac{1}{2}''$.

Appeared serially in *St. Nicholas*, November 1886 to October 1887. Received at the Library of Congress for copyright October 31, 1887.

1888

HOWARD PYLE

(1853–1911)

OTTO / OF THE SILVER HAND / Written and Illustrated by / Howard Pyle / New York / Charles Scribner's Sons / 1888

Collation: brown-coated on white end paper; 2 fly leaves, on the verso of the second is printed an advertisement for Pyle's "Robin Hood"; half title [p. i]; blank [p. ii]; blank [p. iii]; frontispiece [p. iv]; title page [p. v]; copyright notice [p. vi]; table of contents, pp. [vii]–ix; blank [p. x]; list of illustrations, pp. [xi]–xiii; blank [p. xiv]; foreword, pp. [1]–2; text, pp. [3]–170; full page illustration, verso blank [pp. 171–172]; afterword [p. 173]; blank [p. 174], fly leaf; publisher's advertisements, 16 pp. (8 leaves); fly leaf; end paper, as described.

Bound in olive-green cloth with brown leather shelf-back. Front cover is stamped: Otto of the / Silver Hand. Initial *O* of *Otto* is black-stamped on bird ornament in red and green on a gold field; initials of last two words red-stamped, balance of lettering in gold. Below the lettering is a heraldric decoration in red, black and greenish-white with Latin motto in black. At the lower right, in red, is: By / Howard Pyle. Spine is gold-stamped: Otto / of the / Silver / Hand / Howard Pyle. / Scribners   The spine is further decorated with blind-stamped designs.

All edges trimmed. Size of leaf, $8\frac{7}{8}''$ full $\times$ $6\frac{5}{8}''$.

Published November 10, 1888 in an edition of 5,000 copies.

1890

WILLIAM DEAN HOWELLS

(1837–1920)

A BOY'S TOWN / Described for "Harper's Young People" / by / W. D. Howells / Author of "The Shadow of a Dream" "April Hopes" / "A Hazard of New Fortunes" etc. / Illustrated / New York / Harper & Brothers, Franklin Square / 1890

Collation: end paper; 2 fly leaves; inserted frontispiece; title page [p. i]; copyright notice [p. ii]; table of contents [p. iii]; vignette of canal and canal-boat [p. iv]; list of illustrations, pp. [v]–vi; text, pp. [1]–247; blank [p. 248]; fly leaf; end paper.

Bound in twilled blue cloth, stamped in silver and gold. Front cover is gold-stamped: A Boy's Town / W. D. Howells. [*in facsimile autograph*]   The cover is stamped in silver with a border, ornamental stamping at bottom and at upper inner corners. The spine is stamped, lettering in gold, decorations in silver: [*ornament*] / A Boy's / Town / [*ornament*] / W. D. Howells / [*ornament*] / Harpers / [*ornament*]

All edges trimmed. Size of leaf, $7\frac{1}{4}'' \times 4\frac{7}{8}''$. The full-page illustrations as listed are on coated paper and inserted.

The first state of the first edition may be distinguished by the presence of the vignette on the verso of the table of contents leaf; this was later removed to p. 44.

Received at the Library of Congress for copyright October 11, 1890.

1890

SARAH ORNE JEWETT

(1849–1909)

BETTY LEICESTER / a Story for Girls / by / Sarah
Orne Jewett / [*publisher's seal*] / Boston and New
York / Houghton, Mifflin and Company / The River-
side Press, Cambridge / 1890

Collation: end paper; fly leaf, inserted; blank [p. i]; list of
Books by Miss Jewett [p. ii]; title page [p. iii]; copyright
notice dated 1889 [p. iv]; dedication [p. v]; blank [p. vi];
table of contents [p. vii]; blank [p. viii]; text, pp. [1]–287;
blank [p. 288]; fly leaf, inserted; end paper.

Bound in cloth: red shelf-back with white sides. On the
front cover the white cloth is red-stamped: Betty · Leicester /
Sarah · Orne · Jewett   The lettering is stamped against a
background of a chrysanthemum, also in red, extending almost
the entire height of the cover. At the foot of the flower, in
heart-shaped outline, is the monogram OW   The spine is
gold-stamped: Betty / Leicester / S. O. Jewett / Houghton
/ Mifflin . & . Co   Extending from below *Leicester* to
Houghton is a gold-stamped chrysanthemum

Top edges gilt, other edges rough-trimmed. Size of leaf,
$5\frac{15}{16}'' \times 4\frac{1}{4}''$.

Received for copyright at the library of Congress November 14, 1889.

In the first state of the first edition the last title in the list
of books at [p. ii] is "Betty Leicester." In later states the list
is expanded. In addition to the trade edition above collated the
publishers issued a state on large paper.

1891

LAURA ELIZABETH HOWE RICHARDS

(1850–   )

CAPTAIN JANUARY / by / Laura E. Richards / [*decorative rule*] / Boston / Estes & Lauriat / 1891

Collation: end paper; inserted fly leaf; title page, copyright notice on verso dated 1890; table of contents, verso blank; sub-title, verso blank; text, pp. 1–64; fly leaf; end paper.

Bound in grey boards, grained in imitation of leather, with white cloth shelf-back. Front cover is black-stamped: Captain / January / by / . Laura E. Richards. / [*picture of Star Bright*]   To the left of the lettering, which appears on the board, is a lighthouse stamped in black and gold; the latter appears on the cloth. The spine is lettered in sideways fashion and reads from top to bottom: .Captain January.

All edges trimmed. Size of leaf, $7\frac{1}{2}''$ scant $\times$ $5\frac{1}{2}''$ full.

The first state may be identified by the presence of the following notice at the foot of the copyright page: Typography by J. S. Cushing & Co.   Presswork by Berwick & Smith. Estes Press, Boston. No attempt is made here to indicate the pattern in which the notice appears; it does not appear in later printings.

Catalogers have asserted that the first state may be determined by the presence of the word *coseyly* at the end of line 21, p. 8. Since this spelling persists as late as the 18th Thousand it is of no value in identifying the first printing. Of equal little value is the fact that at the same page, line 17, the word *sitting*, in the first printings, was later altered to *setting*. This error continues through several of the early printings.

Received for copyright at the Library of Congress June 28, 1890.

1891

WILLIAM OSBORN STODDARD

(1835–1925)

LITTLE SMOKE / a Tale of the Sioux / by / William O. Stoddard / Author of Crowded Out o' Crofield, etc. / [*arrow-quiver and shield*] / With 14 Full-Page Illustrations and 72 Head and Tail / Pieces Drawn by Frederic S. Dellenbaugh / New York / D. Appleton and Company / 1891

Collation: glazed yellow end paper; inserted fly leaf; inserted frontispiece; title page, copyright notice on verso; table of contents, pp. [1]–2; list of full-page illustrations [p. 3]; blank [p. 4]; list of head and tail pieces, pp. [5]–6; text, pp. [7]–295; blank [p. 296]; 4 pp. publisher's advertisements; fly leaf; inserted fly leaf; end paper, as described.

Noted in both green and blue cloths. Front cover is silver-stamped with an oblong panel, head of boy reading at center, surrounded by floral decorations. At the lower part of the cover is an oblong enclosing: Little Smoke / by / William O. Stoddard   The whole enclosed within a floral border. The spine is silver-stamped: [*floral decoration*] / [*rule*] / Little / Smoke / [*rule*] / [*upright panel of floral decorations*] / [*rule*] / D. Appleton & Co. / [*rule*] / [*floral decoration*]

All edges trimmed. Size of leaf $7\frac{5}{8}''$ full $\times$ $5\frac{5}{8}''$ full. The full page plates as listed at [p. 3] are inserted.

Received for copyright at the Library of Congress October 19, 1891.

1892

CHARLES EDWARD CARRYL

(1842–1920)

THE / ADMIRAL'S CARAVAN / by / Charles E. Carryl / Author of "Davy and the Goblin" / With Illustrations by / Reginald B. Birch / [*publisher's ornament*] / New York / The Century Co. / 1892

Collation: fly leaf; half-title, verso blank; frontispiece, recto blank; title page [p. 1]; copyright notice [p. 2]; dedication [p. 3]; blank [p. 4]; table of contents [p. 5]; blank [p. 6]; list of illustrations [pp. 7–9]; blank [p. 10]; text, pp. [11]–140; fly leaf; lining paper, part of the last signature. The front lining paper is an integral part of the first signature.

Bound in grey cloth stamped in black, gold, white, red and blue. The front cover is lettered with black outline: The Admiral's / Caravan / by / Charles E. Carryl   Decorated with a picture of the Admiral, stork, Noah's ark and toys, all printed in the colors listed above. Spine is lettered in gold outlined with black: The / Admiral's / Caravan / by / Charles / E. / Carryl / [*bird: in red, white and black*] / The / Century / Co   At lower right of back cover is vignette of weeping mouse, two fallen leaves; stamped in black and white.

All edges trimmed. Size of leaf, $8\frac{3}{8}'' \times 6\frac{1}{2}''$.

Appeared serially in *St. Nicholas*, December 1891 to May 1892. Received at the Library of Congress for copyright September 19, 1892.

1893

JAMES OTIS KALER
(James Otis)

(1848–1912)

JENNY WREN'S / BOARDING-HOUSE. / A Story
of Newsboy Life in New York. / by James Otis, /
Author of / "Toby Tyler," "Mr. Stubbs's Brother,"
"Raising the Pearl," etc. / Illustrated by W. A. Rogers.
/ Boston: / Estes and Lauriat, / Publishers. [1893]

Collation: end paper, printed with an all-over floral design; inserted fly leaf; frontispiece [pp. i–ii]; title page
[p. iii]; copyright notice dated 1893 [p. iv]; table of contents, pp. [v]–vi; list of illustrations [p. vii]; blank [p. viii];
sub-title [p. ix]; blank [p. x]; text, pp. [11]–173; blank [p.
174]; fly leaf; end paper, as described.

Noted in both blue and brown cloths, stamped either gold
and blue or gold and black. All lettering in gold; the front
cover reads: Jenny / Wren's / Boarding House / [*decoration
in gold*] / James Otis   At the top of the cover is a gold-
stamped ornamental frame enclosing a blue (or black) vignette
of Jenny together with a gold-stamped rose branch. Cover is
further decorated in black (or blue) with a sparrow, ribbons,
rosettes and rules. Spine gold-lettered: Jenny Wren's Boarding
House [*reading sideways from top to bottom*]

All edges trimmed. Size of leaf $7\frac{13}{16}'' \times 6\frac{1}{4}''$. Frontispiece
and other full page illustrations as listed at [p. vii] are in-
serted.

Appeared serially as "Jenny's Boarding House" in *St. Nicholas* February to August 1887. Received for copyright at the
Library of Congress August 23, 1893.

1894

CHARLES KING

(1844–1933)

CADET DAYS / A Story of West Point / by / Captain Charles King, U. S. A. / Author of / "A War-Time Wooing" "Between the Lines" / "Campaigning With Crook" etc. / Illustrated / [*publisher's seal*] / New York / Harper & Brothers Publishers / 1894

Collation: end paper; fly leaf; inserted frontispiece; title page [p. i]; copyright notice [p. ii]; dedication [p. iii]; blank [p. iv]; list of illustrations, pp. [v]–vi; text, pp. 1–293; blank [p. 294]; publisher's advertisements [pp. 295–296]; end paper.

Bound in twilled West Point blue cloth stamped in gold, silver and black. The front cover is silver-stamped: [*ribbon, on which in cover color:*] West Point / [*the following in silver:*] Cadet Days / by / Captain Charles King   Cover is further stamped with two gold American shield-eagles and, in black, stars and laurel branches. The spine is stamped: [*black star*] / Cadet [*gold*] / Days [*gold*] / [*black star*] / King [*gold*] / [*sword and laurel branch stamped in gold and black*] / Harpers [*gold*]

All edges trimmed. Size of leaf, $7\frac{1}{4}''$ scant $\times$ $4\frac{7}{8}''$. All illustrations as listed at pp. [v]–vi are on coated paper and inserted.

Recorded as received in the *Publishers' Weekly* of May 5, 1894.

1894

EVERETT TITSWORTH TOMLINSON

(1859–1931)

War of 1812 Series / [*rule*] / the / SEARCH FOR
ANDREW FIELD / a Story of the Times of 1812 / by
/ Everett T. Tomlinson / Lee and Shepard Publishers /
10 Milk Street / Boston [1894]

Collation: slate-coated on white end paper; inserted fly
leaf; frontispiece, inserted; title page [p. i]; copyright notice
dated 1894 [p. ii]; preface [p. iii]; blank [p. iv]; table of
contents, pp. [v]–vi; list of illustrations [p. vii]; blank [p.
viii]; text, pp. [9]–313; blank [p. 314]; publisher's advertisements, 6 pp.; inserted fly leaf; end paper, as described.

Bound in red cloth with black and gold stamping. The front
cover is lettered: .War.of.1812.Series. [*in black*] / the
Search [*in black and gold*] / for [*in gold*] / Andrew Field
[*in black and gold*] / Everett T. Tomlinson [*in black*]
Cover decorated with vignette of small sail-boat prow and
figures of boys, stamped in gold and black. The spine is lettered: The / Search / for / Andrew / Field / [*rule*] / Tomlinson / [*vignette of boy in black and gold*] / Lee and Shepard   Title stamped in gold and black with exception of *for*
which is gold; other stamping, except as noted, in black.

All edges trimmed. Size of leaf, 7¼″ × 5″.

Received for copyright at the Library of Congress August
6, 1894.

1894

(MARGARET) MARSHALL SAUNDERS

(1861–   )

BEAUTIFUL JOE / An Autobiography / by Marshall
Saunders / Author of "My Spanish Sailor" / With an
Introduction / by / Hezekiah Butterworth / Editor of
Youth's Companion / [*dog's head*] / Philadelphia /
American Baptist Publication Society / 1420 Chestnut
Street / 1894

Collation: end paper; inserted fly leaf; frontispiece, inserted; title page [p. 1]; copyright notice dated 1893 [p. 2];
dedication, p. 3; *American Humane Education Society Prize
Competition, No. 3* . . . [p. 4]; preface, p. 5; blank [p. 6];
introduction, pp. 7–9; blank [p. 10]; table of contents, pp.
11–12; text, pp. 13–304; inserted fly leaf; end paper.

Bound in mottled blue cloth with gold stamping. The front
cover is stamped: Beautiful Joe / by / Marshall Saunders /
[*reclining dog*]   Spine is stamped: Beautiful / Joe

All edges trimmed. Size of leaf, $7\frac{1}{16}''$ full $\times 4\frac{7}{8}''$. All illustrations, of which there are six including the frontispiece, are
printed on coated paper and inserted.

The first state of the first edition has a frontispiece captioned
in the facsimile autograph of the author: *"Open thy mouth
for the dumb." / Marshall Saunders.*   The picture is that
of the author, seated, offering a ball (it may be a gob of raw
hamburger) to a black and white dog who sits in a begging
position. At lower right corner of the picture is reproduced
the blind-stamped impress of the photographer. The dedication is in five lines, in much later editions the dedication
appears in differing form and text. The book was reissued
with the imprint of Charles H. Banes on the title page, a
frontispiece other than the one described above and with the
note at [p. 4] removed.

(MARGARET) MARSHALL SAUNDERS

The author once stated that the publishers of the first edition supplied her with several sets of untrimmed sheets which were bound in leather for her personal use. The editor has not had the privilege of examining these untrimmed copies.

Recorded as received in the *Publishers' Weekly* of February 3, 1894. Received at the Library of Congress January 8, 1894.

Later printings may occur with one or more features of the first printing but the chief mark of identification is the imprint. Copies with the New York imprint of A. D. F. Randolph, either alone or in combination with the Banes imprint, are late. In later printings the title page describes Hezekiah Butterworth as either *of Youth's Companion* or *Editor of Youth's Companion.*

R. F. Roberts in his re-examination of the first edition of *Beautiful Joe* (published in *The Papers of the Bibliographical Society of America,* Vol. 35, 1941, pp. 74-75), announced that in the earliest printing the reading of the first line, p. 84, is: *but how in . . . ;* later revised to: — *it isn't good . . . ;* that on the title-page Hezekiah Butterworth is described as *Editor of Youth's Companion;* later *of Youth's Companion.* Roberts expresses a preference for the frontispiece captioned *My Name Is . . . ;* and is of the opinion that "the imprint [on the title-page] alone is of no particular bibliographical significance."

1894

KIRK MUNROE

(1850–1930)

THE FUR-SEAL'S TOOTH / A Story of Alaskan Adventure / by / Kirk Munroe / Author of / "Dorymates" "Campmates" "Canoemates" / "Raftmates" etc. / Illustrated / [*publisher's seal*] / New York / Harper & Brothers Publishers / 1894

Collation: end paper; inserted frontispiece; title page [p. i]; copyright notice [p. ii], with list of books by Kirk Munroe; proem [p. iii]; blank [p. iv]; table of contents, pp. [v]–vi; list of illustrations, pp. [vii]–viii; map: *Alaska and Behring Sea,* inserted; text, pp. 1–267; blank [p. 268]; publisher's advertisements, 4 pp.; end paper.

Bound in light green cloth stamped in green, red, blue and black. Front cover red-lettered: The / Fur-Seal's / Tooth / Kirk / Munroe   Front cover decorated with color-stamped necklace of fur-seal's teeth and Alaskan garment. Spine red-lettered: The / Fur-Seal's / Tooth / Kirk / Munroe / [*vignette in red, blue and green: seal on ice-floe*] / Harpers

All edges trimmed. Size of leaf, $7\frac{1}{4}'' \times 4\frac{7}{8}''$. Full page plates as listed are printed on coated paper and inserted.

Received for copyright at the Library of Congress August 25, 1894.

1896

ANNIE FELLOWS JOHNSTON

(1863–1931)

"Cosy Corner Series" / THE LITTLE COLONEL /
by / Annie Fellows-Johnston / Author of "Big Brother"
/ Illustrated by Etheldred B. Barry / [*publisher's monogram*] / Boston / Joseph Knight Company / 1896

Collation: end paper; fly leaf; half-title, verso blank; frontispiece, recto blank; title page, copyright notice on the verso
dated 1895; dedication, verso blank; list of illustrations, verso
blank; text, pp. [1]–102; 3 leaves of publisher's advertisements, the verso of the last blank; end paper.

Bound in green cloth. The front cover is gold-lettered: The
Little Colonel   The front cover is further stamped in green
with an outline shield in which is a black silhouette of the
Little Colonel; ribbons, ornaments and: Cosy Corner Series
Wholly enclosed by double-rule border. Spine is gold-lettered: The / Little / Colonel / [*rule*] / Johnston / [*the
following in green:*] [*floral ornament*] / [*publisher's monogram*]

All edges trimmed. Size of leaf $7\frac{1}{16}''\times4\frac{13}{16}''$. All illustrations as listed are integral parts of the book.

Recorded as received in the *Publishers' Weekly* of December 7, 1895. Received at the Library of Congress November
11, 1895.

1897

JOHN BENNETT

(1865–   )

MASTER SKYLARK / A Story of / Shakspere's Time / [*leaf ornament*] / by / John Bennett / Illustrations by Reginald B. Birch / [*publisher's ornament*] / New York / The Century Co. / 1897

Collation: end paper; half-title [p. i]; blank [p. ii]; frontispiece, inserted; title page [p. iii]; copyright notice [p. iv]; dedication [p. v]; blank [p. vi]; table of contents, pp. vii–viii; list of illustrations, pp. ix–xi; blank [p. xii]; sub-title [p. xiii]; blank [p. xiv]; text, pp. 1–380; end paper.

Bound in light brown cloth. Front cover is stamped in black and red, all lettering red except as noted: Master / Skylark / A Story of [*leaf decoration*] / Shakspere's / Time [*decoration*] / by [*in black*] / John [*in black*] / Bennett [*in black*] / [*leaf decoration*]   To the left of the lettering and extending the entire height of the cover, printed in black, is a sketch of Shakspere and Master Skylark. The spine is black-stamped: Master / Skylark / [*crown*] / [*red and black floral decoration*] / by / John / Bennett / [*decorative rule*] / The Century Co   At the center of the back cover, in red, is stamped Shakspere's monogram.

All edges trimmed. Size of leaf $7\frac{3}{8}'' \times 5\frac{1}{4}''$. The illustrations as listed at pp. ix–xi are full page, printed on coated paper and inserted.

Appeared serially in *St. Nicholas*, November 1896 to October 1897. Received at the Library of Congress for copyright September 17, 1897.

1898

ALBERT BIGELOW PAINE

(1861–1937)

THE HOLLOW TREE / by / Albert Bigelow Paine /
Illustrated by / J. M. Condé / [*publisher's monogram*]
/ New York / R. H. Russell / MDCCCXCVIII [1898]

Collation: end paper; fly leaf [pp. 1–2]; half title [p. 3];
blank [p. 4]; frontispiece, inserted; title page [p. 5]; copyright notice dated 1898 [p. 6]; table of contents [p. 7];
blank [p. 8]; text, pp. [9]–128; end paper.

Bound in cream paper boards with tan buckram shelf-back.
Sides are identically brown-printed with picture of entrance
to the Hollow Tree, opossum, raccoon and crow. The opos-
sum is nailing a sign to the tree; sign is lettered: The Hollow
/ Tree   Below the picture is printed: New York R. H.
Russell Publisher

All edges untrimmed. Size of leaf $9\frac{1}{16}''\times 7''$.

Received at the Library of Congress for copyright October
6, 1898.

1898

ERNEST THOMPSON SETON
(Ernest Seton Thompson)

(1860–   )

. I .

WILD . ANIMALS . HAVE . KNOWN / . *and* . *200. Drawings.* / by / *Ernest* [elk's footprint] *Seton* [elk's footprint] *Thompson* / Naturalist . to . the . Govern / ment . of . Manitoba . . Author . of . / 'Birds . of . Manitoba' [3 birds in silhouette] . / 'Mammals . of . Manitoba' [elk in silhouette] . / 'Art . Anatomy . of . Animals' . / Being the *P*ersonal Histories of / Lobo / Silverspot / *R*aggylug / *B*ingo / *T*he Springfield Fox / *T*he Pacing Mustang / *W*ully / and *R*edruff / [animal skull with horns] / [rule] / Published . by . . *Charles . Scribner's . Sons* . New . York . City . A . D . 1898.   Italicized characters are printed in red. Immediately below the *Wild* of the title is a square vignette of the author, drawing-board in hand, seated below a tree surrounded by animals and birds.

Collation: end paper; 2 blank fly leaves composed of a single sheet folded once to make two leaves; title page [p. 1]; copyright notice [p. 2]; dedication [p. 3]; blank [p. 4]; combined table of contents and list of illustrations, pp. 5–7; blank [p. 8]; note to the reader, pp. 9–13; blank [p. 14]; sub-title [p. 15]; blank [p. 16]; text, pp. 17–358; tail-piece, p. 359; blank [p. 360]; fly leaf; end paper. Pp. 1–4 are printed on a vellum-like paper and are composed of a single sheet folded once to make the four pages.

ERNEST THOMPSON SETON

Bound in green silk-like cloth stamped in gold and black.
. I .

Front cover is gold-lettered: Wild . Animals . Have . Known
/ Ernest Seton Thompson   In black, below the title, are
heads of fox, dog and wolf. Above the title: flying crow;
below title, at extreme left of cover, animal tracks with up-
right rabbitt at foot and artist's initials. Spine is gold-lettered:
Wild / Animals / . I . Have / Known / [*fox-head in black*]
/ Ernest / Seton / Thompson / [*two animal tracks in black*]
/ Scribners

Top edges gilt; other edges untrimmed. Size of leaf, 8″ ×
$5\frac{5}{8}$″. With the exception of the final tail-piece all the illustrations as listed at pp. 5–7 are on coated paper and inserted;
the tail-piece is an integral part of the book.

In the first state of the first edition, p. 265, last paragraph,
is omitted the line: *The Angel whispered don't go.* This was
added to later printings.

Published October 22, 1898, in an edition of 2,000 copies.
Of this number 260 were imprinted for David Nutt, *London*
and 100 copies imprinted for George Morany, *Toronto*.

1899

RALPH HENRY BARBOUR

(1870–)

THE HALF-BACK / a Story of School, / Football, and Golf / by / Ralph Henry Barbour / Illustrated by B. West Clinedinst / [*golf-bag, golf-sticks, baseball bats, balls, etc.*] / New York / D. Appleton and Company / 1899

   Collation: light-brown-coated on white end paper; fly leaf, inserted; frontispiece, inserted; title page [p. i]; copyright notice [p. ii]; dedication [p. iii]; blank [p. iv]; table of contents, p. v; blank [p. vi]; list of illustrations and diagrams [p. vii]; blank [p. viii]; text, pp. 1–267; blank [p. 268]; 4 pp. (2 leaves) publisher's advertisements; fly leaf, inserted; end paper, as described.

   Bound in red or red-orange cloth. The front cover is lettered in dark red outlined in black: The Half-Back / Ralph · H · Barbour / [*figure of running football player in red and black*] Spine is gold-lettered: The / Half-Back / [*rule*] / Barbour / Appletons   Below the author's name is golf-bag, balls, golf-club and baseball bat stamped in dark red and black.

   All edges trimmed. Size of leaf, $7\frac{5}{8}''$ full $\times$ $5\frac{9}{16}''$.

   Illustrations as listed at [p. vii] are inserted; diagrams are integral parts of the book and are textual.

   Received at the *Publishers' Weekly* and recorded in the issue of October 21, 1899. Received at the Library of Congress for copyright September 13, 1899.

1899

WILLIAM ALLEN WHITE

(1868–   )

THE COURT OF / BOYVILLE / by / William Allen White / Author of The Real Issue, etc. / [*publisher's seal*] / New York / Doubleday & McClure Co. / 1899

Collation: end paper; fly leaf; half-title [p. i]; blank [p. ii]; frontispiece [pp. iii–iv]; title page [p. v]; copyright notice [p. vi]; table of contents [p. vii]; 8 lines, poetry [p. viii]; blank [p. ix]; note on the illustrations [p. x]; list of illustrations, pp. xi–xv; blank [p. xvi]; foreword, pp. xvii–xxx; sub-title, p. i; *A Wail in B Minor* [p. 2]; text, pp. 3–358; fly leaf; end paper.

Bound in rough tan buckram, sides identically stamped in green, black, orange and brown. Lettered in orange: The Court / of Boyville / [*vignette: acrobatic boy "showing-off" and disdainful girl*] / William Allen White   Title and author's name enclosed in double-rule boxes. Further decorated with double-rules intersecting and bleeding off cover. Spine orange-lettered: The / Court of / Boyville [*the preceding 3 lines enclosed in double-rule box*] / White [*enclosed in double-rule box*] / Doubleday / & McClure Co. The spine is further decorated with a series of double-rules.

Copies have been noted with all edges trimmed or with the fore- and bottom-edges untrimmed. The above collated copy is of the untrimmed state, the leaves measuring $7\frac{5}{8}'' \times 5''$. All illustrations as listed at pp. xi–xv are on coated paper and inserted.

Recorded as received in the *Publishers' Weekly* of November 4, 1899. Received at the Library of Congress October 21, 1899.

1900

(FRANK) GELETT BURGESS

(1866–   )

GOOPS / AND HOW TO BE THEM / A Manual
of Manners for Polite Infants / Inculcating Many Juvenile Virtues / Both by Precept and Example / With
Ninety Drawings / by Gelett Burgess / [*three Goops*]
/ New York / Frederick A. Stokes Company / Publishers [*1900*] The title page is wholly enclosed by
single rule box.

Collation: end paper; half title, on the verso of which is
a list of three books headed: *Books by Gelett Burgess,* the
last being the "Goops"; title page, copyright notice dated
1900 on the verso; dedication, verso blank; table of contents,
one leaf (2 pp.) ; introduction [p. 1]; picture of three Goops
[p. 2]; text [pp. 3–87]; tail-piece [p. 88]; end paper. The
pages are unnumbered.

Bound in red cloth with black and white stamping. The
front cover is black lettered: Goops / and How to be Them
/ [*the preceding lines are enclosed by single rule box*] /
[*fire-place in black and white with picture of two Goops and
their parents. On the mantel is:* A Manual of Manners /
for Polite Infants   *The whole is enclosed in single rule
box, under which in another box:*] Gelett Burgess   All
three boxes are enclosed by a single-rule box. The spine is
black-stamped: Goops [*flourish*] Burgess   The back cover
is stamped at the center in black and white with two Goops;
cover bordered by black double-rule.

All edges trimmed. Size of leaf, $10\frac{1}{16}$″ $\times$ $7\frac{3}{4}$″ full.

Appeared partially in *St. Nicholas* during 1898 and 1899.
Received at the Library of Congress for copyright August 22,
1900.

1900

LYMAN FRANK BAUM

(1856–1919)

THE WON- / DERFUL / WIZARD / OF / [*to the right of the preceding 4 lines is:*] OZ / by L. Frank Baum / With Pictures by [*in red*] / W. W. Denslow. / [*the 3 lines following are on a yellow field on top of which (in blue, white and red, the latter on the axe-handle) the Tin Woodman and the Scarecrow*] Geo. M. Hill Co. / Chicago. [*in red*] / New York. / 1900 Wholly enclosed by double rule border. The date appears below border. All printing, except as noted, in dark blue. *Oz* is decorated by red printed lion. To left of yellow field is printed Denslow's symbol. With the exception of the date and imprint all lettering appears on a green-printed field.

Collation: issued without end papers; lining paper is drab-brown printed in black with picture of the lion; blank [p. 1]; publisher's advertisement [p. 2]; title page, inserted [pp. 3–4]; introduction [p. 5]; copyright notice dated 1899 [p. 6]; list of chapters [p. 7]; dedication [p. 8]; sub-title page for Chapter I [p. 9]; blank [p. 10]; text, pp. [11]–259; blank [p. 260]; text of Chapter XXIV [p. 261]; blank [p. 262] lining paper, for further description of which see below.

Note: The book was issued without end papers in the strictest and technical sense of the word, *i.e.,* the lining paper pasted to the front cover is not conjugate with the first leaf; the last leaf is not conjugate with the lining paper pasted to the back cover.

Bound in green cloth stamped in red and green. The lettering is in both red and green; green is here indicated in roman face, red lettering in italics. The front cover is stamped:

LYMAN FRANK BAUM

The *Wonder- / ful Wizard* / of Oz / by / L. Frank Baum /
Pictures by / W. W. Denslow / [*green field on which in
green, red and cover color is stamped a picture of the lion*].
The spine is lettered: The / Wonder- / ful / Wizard / of
Oz / [*red sea horse decoration*] / Baum / [*green field on
which in red, green and cover color is stamped a picture of
the dog*] / *Geo. M. Hill Co.*   Back cover is stamped: The
Wonder- / ful Wizard / of Oz / [*green field on which in red
and cover color are pictures of Dorothy, Tin Woodman and
Scarecrow. In cover color: a small "sun"; in cover color and
green: a wisp of straw extending from Scarecrow's head.*]

All edges trimmed. Size of leaf, $8\frac{3}{8}'' \times 6\frac{1}{2}''$.

Received at the *Publishers' Weekly* office and recorded in
the issue of June 9, 1900. Received at the Library of Congress
December 12, 1900. A revised edition was received at the
Library of Congress August 20, 1903.

In addition to the tipped-in title page (printed in color on
lightly coated paper) there are 23 full page color plates inserted as follows: pp. 14 (or at p. 12), 20, 34, 36, 44, 56, 66,
80, 92, 102, 114, 126, [138], 150, 160, 170, 184, 198, 212,
220, 228, 246, 254.

The first edition is distinguished by the following features:
on the spine the publisher's name is printed from an unorna-
mented type; the *Co.* is set in ordinary fashion. Publisher's advertisements at [p. 2] are enclosed by a single-rule border.
P. 14, line 1, reads: *low wail on . . . ;* later: *low wail of
. . .* P. 81, 4th line from the bottom, *peices* for *pieces.* The
colophon at the terminal lining paper is in eleven lines, the
initial letter in color, the whole enclosed by a box and with a
color ornament at the left of the lettering. The earliest copies
have perfect type at p. 100, last line; also at the last line of
p. 186.

In addition to the above collated first edition there are at
least two other states which for convenience shall be termed
States Y and Z.

LYMAN FRANK BAUM

State Y: The publisher's name on the spine is printed from seraf'd type; the *Co.* is composed of a single unit with the *C* encircling the *O*. The advertisements are bordered as in the first state collated above; the typographical errors are present at pp. 14 and 81; the colophon at the terminal lining paper has been reset and appears in 13 lines, with no border, no ornamentation and printed entirely in black. The type defects are not present at pp. 100 and 186.

State Z: Publisher's name on the spine appears as in State Y. The advertisements are not enclosed by a box. The typographical errors have been corrected. The type defects are present at pp. 100 and 186.

In addition to the three definite states collated above the book appears with the title page in four known states. In view of the fact that the title page is not an integral part of the book and is a tipped-in leaf it is difficult to assert any definite priority. However, logically the order is as follows:

A: With no copyright notice on the reverse of title page.
B: With copyright notice rubber-stamped on reverse of title page.
C and D: With the copyright notice press-printed from type. In these copies the notice appears in one of two faces: one with the capital *R* having a tail that extends below the line; the other having tails that are on a line with the rest of the printing. Thus far no priority has been established for the long-tail or the short-tail school.

The copy collated in full above carries a contemporary presentation inscription from the author and has no copyright notice on the reverse of the title page.

Since the law requires that copyright notices appear on the verso of the title page it would seem that the publishers, unaware of this requirement, had issued copies without the notice at the proper place. In order to remedy this defect they rubber-stamped copies on hand, later press-printing from type the unbound title pages. However, since the title page is not an integral part of the book it will be wise to give more consideration to the typographical errors at pp. 14 and 81 and to the unbroken type at pp. 100 and 186.

1901

ALICE CALDWELL HEGAN RICE

(1870–   )

MRS. WIGGS OF THE / CABBAGE PATCH / by / Alice Caldwell Hegan / [*vignette: the cabbage-patch*] / Published by the Century Co. / New York . . MCMI

Collation: end paper; fly leaf; half title, verso blank; title page, copyright notice on the verso; dedication, verso blank; table of contents, verso blank; sub-title [p. 1]; blank [p. 2]; text, pp. 3–153; blank [p. 154]; end paper.

Bound in olive-green cloth stamped in black, gold and red-orange. The front cover is stamped at the top with a country wayside scene in cover color, black and gold sky. Below this, to the left, is a stamped figure of Mrs. Wiggs in red-orange, black and cover-color. At bottom of front cover, gold-stamped, is: Mrs. Wiggs / of / the Cabbage Patch / Alice Caldwell Hegan [*in autograph facsimile*]   The spine is gold-lettered: Mrs. / Wiggs / of the / Cabbage / Patch / Hegan / The / Century / Co.

Top edges trimmed, other edges rough-trimmed. Size of leaf, $6\frac{15}{16}''$ scant $\times\ 4\frac{1}{2}''$.

The first state of the binding may be distinguished by the gold sky of the front cover; later bindings have the sky white-stamped.

Received at the Library of Congress September 25, 1901.

1901

JOSEPHINE DIEBITSCH PEARY

(1863–   )

THE SNOW BABY / a True Story with / True Pictures. By / Josephine Diebitsch Peary / [*the four lines
preceding are enclosed in a single-rule box*] / [*circular
picture of the Snow Baby; enclosed in large box*] /
New York. Frederick A. / Stokes Company. Publishers
[1901] [*the two preceding lines are enclosed in a single-rule box*] All the preceding enclosed in single-rule
box.

Collation: end paper; half-title [p. 1]; blank [p. 2]; frontispiece, recto blank [pp. 3–4]; title page [p. 5]; copyright
notice stating *Published October, 1901* [p. 6]; dedication [p.
7]; blank [p. 8]; text, pp. 9–84; end paper.

Bound in light blue cloth with white lettering. The front
cover is lettered: The Snow Baby / [*rule*] / [*Arctic scene in
white, light brown and cover color; at the center is pasted a
picture of the Snow Baby*] / [*rule*] / Josephine D. Peary /
The whole is enclosed by a single-rule box. The rules referred
to extend the entire width of the box.

All edges trimmed. Size of leaf, $10\frac{1}{16}''\times7\frac{3}{4}''$ full.

Appeared originally in *St. Nicholas*, March, 1901, as
"Ahnighito." Received for copyright at the Library of Congress October 21, 1901.

1902

JOHN BENNETT

(1865–   )

BARNABY LEE / by / John Bennett / Author of
"Master Skylark" / With Illustrations by / Clyde O.
De Land / [*publisher's ornament*] / New York / The
Century Co. / 1902

Collation: end paper; fly leaf; half-title [p. i]; blank [p.
ii]; frontispiece, inserted; title page [p. iii]; copyright notice
stating *Published October, 1902* [p. iv]; dedication [p. v];
blank [p. vi]; table of contents, pp. [vii]–viii; list of illustrations, pp. [ix]–x; sub-title [p. 1]; blank [p. 2]; text, pp.
3–454; end paper.

Bound in blue cloth stamped with gold, white and yellow.
The front cover is lettered: Barnaby Lee [*in gold, initials in
yellow with flourishes and outline in gold; enclosed in single-
rule yellow-stamped box*] / John Bennett [*in gold*]   The
author's name appears at the foot of a box that is symmetrically
stamped with an arrangement of windmill-sails in white and
beavers silhouetted in yellow. At the lower right, in white, is
the monogram *DD.* Wholly enclosed by yellow-stamped single-
rule. Both boxes are enclosed by single-rule yellow-stamped
border. Spine is stamped: [*yellow double rule*] / Barnaby /
Lee [*both the preceding are gold-stamped save for the initials
which are yellow and gold*] / [*yellow double rule*] / Bennett
[*gold-stamped*] / The / Century / Co [*publisher's imprint in
gold*] / [*yellow double rule*]   The spine is decorated with
an orderly arrangement of windmill-sails and beavers as described on the front cover.

All edges trimmed. Size of leaf, $7\frac{1}{2}'' \times 5\frac{3}{8}''$. Illustrations
as listed at pp. [ix]–x are on coated paper and inserted.

Appeared serially in *St. Nicholas,* November 1900, to April
1902. Received for copyright at the Library of Congress September 16, 1902.

1902

WILLIAM DEAN HOWELLS

(1837–1920)

THE FLIGHT [*in red*] / OF PONY BAKER [*in red*] / A Boy's Town Story / by / W. D. Howells / Author of / "A Boy's Town" / "Christmas Every Day" etc. / Illustrated / [*publisher's seal*] / New York and London / Harper & Brothers / Publishers 1902 Title page wholly enclosed by single rule box.

Collation: end paper; fly leaf; frontispiece, inserted; title page [p. i]; copyright notice stating *Published September, 1902* [p. ii]; table of contents, pp. iii–[iv]; list of illustrations p. v; blank [p. vi]; sub-title [p. 1]; blank [p. 2]; text, pp. 3–[223]; blank [p. 224]; end paper.

Bound in red cloth with stamping in silver and black. Front cover silver-stamped: The Flight of / Pony Baker / W. D. Howells. Further decorated with black-stamped picture of Pony, path, house, etc. Entirely enclosed by single-rule box and with horizontal rules enclosing title and author's name. Spine is silver-stamped: The / Flight / of / Pony / Baker / [*black rule*] / Howells / [*black rule*] / Harpers   Wholly enclosed by single-rule border in black.

All edges trimmed. Size of leaf $7\frac{1}{8}''$ $\times$ $4\frac{3}{4}''$. Frontispiece and full-page illustrations as listed at p. v are on coated paper and inserted.

Received at the Library of Congress September 26, 1902.

1902

HENRY AUGUSTUS SHUTE

(1856–   )

THE / REAL DIARY / OF A / REAL BOY / [*double-rule*] / [*flower ornament*] / by / Henry A. Shute / [*double-rule*] / The Everett Press / Boston, Mass., Mcmii [1902] Wholly enclosed by a double-rule border. The horizontal rules described above extend the entire width of the enclosing box.

Collation: end paper; title page [p. i]; copyright notice [p. ii]; introduction, pp. iii–v; blank [p. vi]; text, pp. 1–135; blank [p. 136]; fly leaf; end paper.

Bound in green cloth. The front cover is lettered: The *Real* / Diary of a / *Real* / *Boy* / by / Henry /A. Shute / [*to the left of the last 4 lines is a floral decoration, stem and leaves in green, blossom in red*]   All stamping green except as noted by the use of italics, the latter lettering appearing in red. Wholly enclosed by crude green-stamped border. The spine is green-lettered: The / Real / Diary / of a / Real / Boy / Henry / A / Shute / [*flower stamped in green and red*] / The / Everett / Press / Co / Boston

Top edges trimmed, other edges untrimmed. Size of leaf, $6\frac{1}{4}'' \times 4\frac{1}{4}''$.

Received at the Library of Congress November 17, 1902.

This title, the first in an all too short series, was followed by a sequel, "Sequil, or Things Which Aint Finished in the First," *Boston,* 1904.

1903

JACK (JOHN GRIFFITH) LONDON

(1876–1916)

THE CALL / OF THE WILD / by / Jack London / [*dog's head*] / New York / The Macmillan Company / London: Macmillan & Co., Ltd. / 1903 / All Rights Reserved   Printed in black on a light green-blue background of mountain snow scene, enclosed in double-rule box. At the top, between the rules of the border, also in green-blue, is: *Illustrated by Philip R. Goodwin / and Charles Livingston Bull*   At the bottom, in a similar position, in green-blue, appears: *Decorated by Chas. Edw. Hooper.*

Collation: end paper, printed in green-blue with dog-team scene [pp. 1–2]; half-title [p. 3]; publisher's monogram [p. 4]; frontispiece, in color, inserted [pp. 5–6]; title page [p. 7]; copyright notice stating: *Set up, electrotyped, and published July, 1903.* [p. 8]; table of contents, p. 9; blank [p. 10]; list of illustrations, pp. 11–12; sub-title [p. 13]; full-page illustration printed in green-blue [p. 14]; text, pp. 15–231; blank [p. 232]; 2 pp. (one leaf) publisher's advertisements; end paper, as described.

Bound in vertically-ribbed green cloth; stamped in gold, red, white and black. The front cover is gold-lettered: The Call / of the Wild / by / Jack London   In addition to the lettering there are three scenes in red, black and white depicting dog-teams, etc. The spine is gold-stamped: The / Call / of the / Wild / [*oblong decoration: dog, stamped in red, white and black*] / Jack / London / The Macmillan / Company

Top edges gilt, other edges untrimmed. Size of leaf, $7\frac{5}{8}''$ × $5\frac{3}{16}''$. The full-page illustrations in the text are printed in color and inserted. Throughout the book are scattered textual illustrations in color; these are printed on coated paper and are either bound or tipped-in. Each chapter is preceded by a divisional sub-title page on the verso of which a full page illustration is printed in green-blue.

The first binding is of vertically ribbed cloth.

At the time this volume goes to press my good friend, David A. Randall, reports discovery of an unrecorded and hitherto unknown state of this volume. In printed grey wrappers and unillustrated, the publishers are unable to supply any information regarding it. The text differs from that of the published edition. Since this freak (for want of a better word) was discovered in England it is quite possible that it was intended as a reading copy sent for the consideration of the English publishers and is composed of pre-publication sheets.

Received at the Library of Congress July 10, 1903.

1903

KATE DOUGLAS (SMITH) WIGGIN

(1856–1923)

REBECCA / OF SUNNYBROOK / FARM / by / Kate Douglas Wiggin [*the preceding 5 lines enclosed in single-rule box, top of which is picture of the brick-house*] / Boston and New York / Houghton, Mifflin and Company / The Riverside Press, Cambridge / 1903 [*the preceding 4 lines enclosed in single rule box*] Entire title page enclosed in single-rule box. All lettering black; balance green.

Collation: end paper; fly leaf; leaf: recto blank, verso printed with publisher's list; half-title [p. i]; blank [p. ii]; title page [p. iii]; copyright notice with statement *Published October 1903* [p. iv]; dedication [p. v]; blank [p. vi]; 6 lines from Wordsworth [p. vii]; blank [p. viii]; table of contents, pp. [ix]–x; sub-title [p. 1]; blank [p. 2]; text, pp. [3]–327; printer's imprint [p. 328]; fly leaf; end paper.

Bound in green cloth. Stamped in henna, green, white and blue. Front cover is green lettered: Rebecca / of / Sunnybrook Farm / Kate Douglas Wiggin   Above the lettering is a picture of the brick-house; below the lettering is a picture of the brook. Wholly enclosed by double-rule border, inner rules intersecting at the corners. Spine green lettered: Rebecca / of / Sunnybrook / Farm / Kate / Douglas / Wiggin / Houghton / Mifflin & Co.   Spine is decorated with a series of horizontal rules and hollyhocks.

The first state of the binding has the publisher's imprint at the foot of the spine stamped from type $\frac{1}{16}$" high; later states are stamped from type about $\frac{1}{8}$" high. The color stamping has been noted in varying tones but it is not likely that this constitutes a point of issue. All edges trimmed. Size of leaf, $7\frac{1}{4}$" full × $4\frac{7}{8}$".

Received at the Library of Congress September 24, 1903.

1906

JACK (JOHN GRIFFITH) LONDON

(1876–1916)

WHITE FANG / by / Jack London / Author of "The Call of the Wild," "The/ Sea Wolf," etc., etc. / New York / The Macmillan Company / London: Macmillan & Co., Ltd. / 1906 / All rights reserved

Collation: end paper, printed with vignettes in brown-orange; half title [p. i]; list of books by Jack London [p. ii]; colored frontispiece, inserted; title page [p. iii]; copyright notice stating *Published October, 1906.* [p. iv]; table of contents, pp. v–vi; list of illustrations, p. vii; blank [p. viii]; sub-title [p. ix]; blank [p. x]; full page illustration of mountain, printed in brown-orange [p. 1]; blank [p. 2]; text, pp. 3–327; blank [p. 328]; 4 pp. publisher's advertisements, inserted; end paper, as described.

onion skin

Bound in slate-blue vertically ribbed cloth stamped in white, gold and blue-black. Front cover is white-lettered: White / Fang / Jack London   At the center is an upright oblong vignette of wolf and snow scene in blue-black, white and cover color; below, at the lower right corner, in blue-black, is the artist's monogram. The spine is gold-stamped: [*rule*] / White / Fang / London / The Macmillan / Company / [*rule*]

Top and bottom edges trimmed, fore-edge rough trimmed. Size of leaf, $7\frac{7}{16}''$ ×5". Top edges stained yellow. The full-page illustrations in color are inserted. The book is divided into five parts, each preceded by a full page, part of the signature, illustration printed in brown-orange.

Appeared serially in *Outing Magazine,* May to October, 1906. Book received at the Library of Congress October 2, 1906.

122

JACK (JOHN GRIFFITH) LONDON

Although the book is printed on laid paper the title page in all examined copies of the first edition is a cancel leaf of either laid or wove paper. No satisfactory explanation for this has been reached but the printer's file copy, bound in printed paper wrappers, has the title page dated 1905 and bound in as part of the first signature. In view of this it is highly probable that the book, already printed and folded, dated 1905, was delayed in publication in order that the story might have its serial magazine appearance. If such is the case it is obvious that the title page would of necessity require alteration.

Ill. Charles Livingston Bull

LUCY MAUD MONTGOMERY

(1874–   )

NOT AT CHPU

ANNE OF GREEN / GABLES / [*rule*] / by / L. M.
Montgomery / [*rule*] / Illustrated by / M. A. and
W. A. J. Claus / [*rule*] / [*two lines from Browning*]
/ [*publisher's seal*] / [*rule*] / Boston [*ornament*]
L. C. Page & / Company [*ornament*] MDCCCCVIII
[1908]   Wholly enclosed by double-rule box; rules
described above extend the entire width of the enclosing box.

Collation: end paper, half title [p. i]; blank [p. ii]; frontispiece, inserted; title page [p. iii]; copyright notice stating
First Impression, April, 1908 [p. iv]; dedication [p. v]; blank
[p. vi]; table of contents, pp. vii–viii; list of illustrations [p.
ix]; blank [p. x]; text, pp. 1–429; blank [p. 430]; *From
L. C. Page & Company's Announcement List of New Fiction*,
pp. [1]–4; *Selections From L. C. Page and Company's List of
Fiction*, pp. [1]–4; end paper.

Bound in vertically ribbed ecru cloth. Front cover is gold-
lettered: Anne of / Green Gables / by / L. M. Montgomery
Above the lettering is pasted a bordered square picture of
Anne. The cover is further decorated by a double-rule blind-
stamped border and rule arrangements enclosing picture and
lettering. The spine is gilt-lettered: Anne / of / Green /
Gables / [*rule*] / Montgomery / Page / [*rule*] / Boston
The top and bottom of spine blind-stamped with double-rules.

Top edges trimmed; other edges rough-trimmed. Size of
leaf, $7\frac{1}{2}''\times 5\frac{1}{8}''$. Illustrations as listed are full page, printed
on coated paper and are inserted.

Received at the Library of Congress June 12, 1908.

1908

PETER (SHEAF HERSHEY) NEWELL

(1862–1924)

THE HOLE BOOK / by Peter Newell / [*ink-blot* *"man"*] / Harper & Brothers / New York [1908] The foregoing is black-printed on an orange field of heads and such watching the antics of the ink-blot man.

Collation: end paper; title page, copyright notice on verso stating *Published October, 1908.*; sub-title, text beginning on verso and followed by 24 leaves, the recto of each printed with an illustration in color and with text on the verso. A feature of each illustration (with the exception of the last) is the hole caused (as no reader dares doubt) by the pistol-ball fired by young Tom Potts in the first picture. The pages are not numbered nor is the book bound in the usual manner; each leaf is a separate sheet and the book is composed of these, held together by metal staples; end paper.

Bound in blue cloth. On the front cover is pasted a color print lettered: The Hole Book / Peter Newell / [*decoration*] The preceding is in black on an orange field. To the left, on a blue field, is depicted a line of children, the first of whom peers through the famous hole, here pictured rather than actual.

All edges trimmed. Size of leaf, $8\frac{11}{16}''$ scant $\times$ $7\frac{3}{16}''$.

Received at the Library of Congress October 15, 1908.

1908

EMERSON HOUGH

(1857–1923)

THE / YOUNG ALASKANS / by / Emerson Hough / Author of / "The Story of the Cowboy" / "The Mississippi Bubble" / etc. etc. / Illustrated / [*publisher's seal*] / Harper & Brothers Publishers / New York and London / MCMVIII [1908] Wholly enclosed by double-rule border with pine-cone decoration at each inner corner.

Collation: end paper; fly leaf; frontispiece, inserted; title page, copyright notice on verso stating *Published October, 1908*; table of contents, 2 pp.; list of illustrations, verso blank; sub-title, verso blank; text, pp. 1–[292]; fly leaf; end paper.

Bound in orange-brown cloth stamped with black and white. Front cover is white-stamped: The Young / Alaskans Cover is further stamped with picture of two boys gaffing a fish; stamped white and black. Spine white-lettered: The / Young /Alaskans / [*bird and net, white and black-stamped*] / Hough / Harpers

All edges trimmed. Size of leaf, $7\frac{5}{16}''\times 5''$.

Received at the Library of Congress for copyright October 22, 1908.

1909

FRANCES BOYD CALHOUN

(?–?)

MISS MINERVA AND / WILLIAM GREEN HILL /   *CML*
by / Frances Boyd Calhoun / [*ornament*] / Illustrated
by / Angus Macdonall / Chicago / The Reilly & Britton Co. / 1909

Collation: end paper; half-title, verso blank; frontispiece,
inserted; title page [p. 1]; copyright notice [p. 2]; table of
contents [pp. 3–4]; text, pp. 5–212; end paper. Pp. 209–
212 constitute one signature, inserted.

Bound in red cloth. Lettering in black and white. Front
cover is white-lettered: Miss Minerva and / William Green
Hill / [*picture in white, black and cover color: Miss Minerva,
lamp in hand, surveying William's clothing which is scattered
on the floor*] /   The spine is white-lettered except as noted:
Miss / Minerva / and / William / Green / Hill / Calhoun
[*in black*] / Reilly & / Britton

Bottom edges untrimmed, other edges trimmed. Size of leaf,
$6\frac{3}{4}''$ full $\times$ $4\frac{1}{2}''$ scant. All illustrations, save the frontispiece,
are integral parts of the book.

Recorded as received for entry in the *Cumulative Book
Index* of February 6, 1909. Received at the Library of Congress February 1, 1909.

1910

OWEN (McMAHON) JOHNSON

(1878–   )

CMU THE VARMINT / by / Owen Johnson / Author of "Arrows of the Almighty," "Max / Fargus," "The Eternal Boy," etc. / [*vignette: running boy in base-ball suit*] / New York / The Baker & Taylor Company / 1910   Enclosed in triple rule border.

onion skin

Collation: end paper; half-title [p. 1]; publisher's advertisements [p. 2]; frontispiece, inserted; title page [p. 3]; copyright notice stating *Published, July, 1910* [p. 4]; dedication [p. 5]; blank [p. 6]; list of illustrations [p. 7]; blank [p. 8]; sub-title [p. 9]; blank [p. 10]; text, pp. 11–396; 2 fly leaves; end paper.

Bound in vertically-ribbed green cloth with orange and black stamping. Front cover is black-lettered: The Varmint / by / Owen Johnson / [*rule*] / [*picture in black and orange: crowd of boys carrying one of their fellows*]   Wholly enclosed by single-rule box. The rule below the author's name extends the entire width of the box, losing itself in the trees at the upper right of the vignette. Spine is orange-lettered: The / Varmint / Johnson / The Baker & / Taylor Co.

All edges trimmed. Size of leaf, $7\frac{5}{16}'' \times 4\frac{7}{8}''$. All illustrations listed at [p. 7] are on coated paper and inserted.

Received at the Library of Congress July 7, 1910.

CMU Has 2nd Issue $20.00

1911

OWEN (McMAHON) JOHNSON

(1878–   )

THE / TENNESSEE SHAD / Chronicling the Rise and Fall of the Firm / of Doc Macnooder and the Tennessee Shad / by / Owen Johnson / Author of "The Varmint," "The Prodigious / Hickey," "The Humming Bird," etc. / [*vignette: standing boy*] / New York / The Baker & Taylor Company / 1911 Wholly enclosed by triple-rule border.

Collation: end paper; half title, publisher's advertisements on the verso; frontispiece, inserted; title page [p. 1]; copyright notice stating *Published May, 1911* [p. 2]; dedication [p. 3]; blank [p. 4]; table of contents [p. 5]; blank [p. 6]; list of illustrations [p. 7]; blank [p. 8]; sub-title [p. 9]; blank [p. 10]; text, pp. 11–307; blank [p. 308]; publisher's advertisements, 4 pp. (2 leaves); fly leaf; end paper.

Bound in red cloth with black and white stamping. White-lettered on the front cover: The / Tennessee / Shad / [*vignette: the Tennessee Shad in a wheelbarrow pushed by Skinner, stamped in white and black*] / Owen / Johnson   The spine is white-lettered: The / Tennessee / Shad / [*vignette: boy, stamped in black and white*] / Johnson / The Baker & / Taylor Co.

All edges trimmed. Size of leaf, $7\frac{5}{16}'' \times 4\frac{7}{8}''$. Illustrations as listed at [p. 7] are on coated paper and inserted.

Received at the Library of Congress May 20, 1911.

1912

(ALICE) JEAN WEBSTER

(1876–1916)

DADDY-LONG-LEGS / by / Jean Webster / With Illustrations / by the Author / [*sketch of "Daddy" and dog*] / New York / The Century Co. / 1912 *on title page*
Wholly enclosed by double-rule box.

Collation: end paper; fly leaf; half-title, publisher's list on the verso; title page, copyright notice on the verso stating: *Published October, 1912;* dedication, verso blank; sub-title [p. 1]; blank [p. 2]; text, pp. 3–304; end paper.

Bound in blue cloth. Front cover green-lettered: Daddy-Long-Legs / Jean / Webster   Decorated with heart shaped ornament with leaves and roses stamped in green and white. Spine green-lettered: Daddy / Long-Legs / [*decoration of roses in white and green*] / Webster / The / Century / Co.

Top edges trimmed, other edges rough trimmed. Size of leaf, $6\frac{13}{16}'' \times 4\frac{1}{2}''$.

Appeared originally as a serial in the *Ladies Home Journal,* April to September, 1912. Received for copyright at the Library of Congress during the month of October, 1912.

1913

ELEANOR HODGMAN PORTER

(1868–1920)

POLLYANNA / [*rule*] / by / Eleanor H. Porter / Author of "Miss Billy," "Miss Billy's Decision," / "Cross Currents," "The Turn of the Tides," etc. / [*rule*] / Illustrated by / Stockton Mulford / [*rule*] / [*publisher's seal*] / [*rule*] / Boston [*ornament*] L. C. Page & / Company [*ornament*] MDCCCCXIII [1913] Wholly enclosed in double-rule box.

Collation: end paper; half title [p. i]; *Works of Eleanor H. Porter* [p. ii]; inserted frontispiece; title page [p. iii]; copyright notice [p. iv] stating: *First Impression, February, 1913;* dedication [p. v]; blank [p. vi]; table of contents, pp. vii–viii; list of illustrations [p. ix]; blank [p. x]; text, pp. 1–310; publisher's advertisements, 16 pp.; end paper.

Bound in pink satin-like cloth, watered. The front cover is gold-stamped: Polly- / Anna [*in decorative box*] / Eleanor H. Porter   Spine is gold-stamped: [*decorative rule*] / Polly- / Anna / [*decorative rule*] / Porter / Page / [*rule*] / Boston

All edges trimmed. Size of leaf, $7\frac{1}{2}''$ scant $\times$ $5\frac{1}{8}''$.

Received for copyright at the Library of Congress February, 1913.

1914

(NEWTON) BOOTH TARKINGTON

(1869–   )

PENROD / by Booth / Tarkington / [*vignette: Penrod and his dog*] / Illustrated by / Gordon Grant / Garden City New York / Doubleday, Page & Company / 1914

Collation: end paper; half title [p. i]; frontispiece [p. ii]; title page [p. iii]; copyright notice [p. iv]; dedication [p. v]; list of *books by the same author* [p. vi]; table of contents, pp. [vii]–viii; list of illustrations [pp. ix–x]; sub-title [p. 1]; blank [p. 2]; text, pp. 3–345; printer's seal and imprint [p. 346]; end paper.

Bound in blue meshed cloth stamped in white and black; all lettering in white. Front cover stamped: Penrod / Booth Tarkington / [*circular vignette in white and black: Penrod sitting on fence, his dog at foot of fence*]   Spine lettered: Penrod / [*leaf decoration*] / Tarkington / Doubleday / Page & Co.

All edges trimmed. Size of leaf, $7\frac{3}{8}''\times5\frac{1}{16}''$.

The earliest printed copies may be distinguished by the presence of the numeral *viii* at the foot of that page; later copies, though possibly of the first printing, have the numeral either partially or wholly removed. The first state is also distinguished by *sence* for *sense*, p. 19, first word, third line from bottom; this error was corrected sometime after the first copies had been printed. The first state of the binding is meshed cloth; later ribbed cloth.

One of the chapters in the volume, "An Overwhelming Saturday," was first published in *Cosmopolitan*, November, 1913, and was issued in pamphlet form, *New York* [1913].

(NEWTON) BOOTH TARKINGTON

Published March 26, 1914; the publishers state that copies in leather were not published before November of the same year.

Appeared in short story form in *Everybody's*, June, 1913; *Saturday Evening Post,* June 21, 1913; and in *Cosmopolitan*, October to December, 1913, inclusive, and January to April, 1914, inclusive.

1914

EDGAR RICE BURROUGHS

(1875–   )

TARZAN / OF THE / APES / Chicago / A. C.
McClurg & Co. / 1914 / Edgar Rice Burroughs
Wholly enclosed by single-rule box which contains a
silhouette of Tarzan, trees, vines, etc. Imprint and date
are enclosed in single rule box.

Collation: end paper; fly leaf; half-title, verso blank; title
page, copyright notice on the verso stating *Published June,
1914*; dedication, verso blank; table of contents, one leaf,
printed on recto only, verso blank; text, pp. 1–[401]; blank
[p. 402]; 2 fly leaves; end paper.

*CMU has
maroon
cloth*

Noted in both maroon and green cloth. Gold-stamped on
the front cover: Tarzan of the / Apes / Edgar Rice Burroughs /   Enclosed by double-rule box, blind-stamped,
broken at the left by the *T* in *Tarzan* and at the right by the
S in *Apes.* The spine is gold-stamped: [*rule*] / Tarzan / of
the / Apes / [*rule*] / Burroughs / A. C. McClurg / & Co.
/ [*rule*]

Copies have been noted as collated above or with the publisher's acorn ornament added at the foot of the spine; no
priority for either state has been determined.

All edges trimmed. Size of leaf, $7\frac{5}{16}''$ × $4\frac{7}{8}''$.

Received at the Library of Congress June 20, 1914.

1916

(NEWTON) BOOTH TARKINGTON

(1869–   )

PENROD AND SAM / by / Booth Tarkington / Author of "Penrod" / [*publisher's seal*] / Illustrated by / Worth Brehm / Garden City New York / Doubleday, Page & Company / 1916   Wholly enclosed by double rule box.

Collation: end paper; half-title [p. i]; list of books *by the same author* [p. ii]; frontispiece, inserted; title page [p. iii]; copyright notice [p. iv]; dedication [p. v]; blank [p. vi]; table of contents, pp. vii–viii; list of illustrations, p. ix; blank [p. x]; sub-title [p. 1]; blank [p. 2]; text, pp. 3–356; end paper.

Bound in green cloth with white and black stamping. Front cover is white-lettered: Penrod / and Sam / Booth Tarkington / [*vignette in black on white field: Penrod, Sam and Verman, the latter seated on the floor of Sister Margaret's closet*] Spine is white-lettered save for the publisher's name which is black-stamped: Penrod / and / Sam / [*leaf decoration*] / Tarkington / Doubleday / Page & Co.

All edges trimmed. Size of leaf, $7\frac{3}{8}'' \times 4\frac{15}{16}''$. Illustrations as listed at p. ix are on coated paper and inserted. The earliest printed copies have perfect type at several places throughout the book; most noticeably at pp. 86, 141, 144, 149 and 210.

A few copies of this volume have been noted printed on an appreciably thinner paper and with narrower margins, bound in a ribbed blue cloth similar to that of the second state "Penrod" binding. The exact status of such copies is not known but two theories have been advanced: that the binding was an attempt to produce a volume that would serve as a uniform companion to "Penrod"; that the publishers attempted to produce the book at a lower price for the "drug-store" trade. Thus far no substantiation for either theory has been produced.

Published October 1916. Appeared serially in *Cosmopolitan*, during 1915 and 1916.

1917

DOROTHY CANFIELD
(Dorothea Frances Canfield Fisher)

(1879–   )

UNDERSTOOD BETSY / by / Dorothy Canfield / Author of "The Bent Twig," etc. / Illustrations by / Ada C. Williamson / [*publisher's ornament*] / New York / Henry Holt and Company / 1917

Collation: end paper; inserted frontispiece; title page, copyright notice on verso stating *Published August, 1917*; table of contents leaf, verso blank; list of illustrations leaf, verso blank; text, pp. [1]–271; blank [p. 272] blank fly leaf; 8 pp. (four leaves) publisher's advertisements; end paper.

Bound in green cloth with black and green stamping. Front cover is black-lettered: Understood / Betsy / by Dorothy Canfield /   Below author's name is double rule extending full width of double-rule box bordering cover; below double rules is a series of silhouettes of cats, butterflies, cat-o'-nine tails. All decorative stamping in green. Spine is black-stamped: [*double-rule*] / Understood / Betsy / [*rule*] / Canfield / [*cat's head*] / Henry Holt / and Company

All edges trimmed. Size of leaf, $7\frac{3}{8}'' \times 5''$. All illustrations as listed are on coated paper and inserted.

Appeared serially in *St. Nicholas*, November 1916, to July 1917. Received at the Library of Congress September 1, 1917.

1920

HUGH LOFTING

(1886–   )

THE / [*flourish*] STORY OF [*flourish*] / DOCTOR
DOLITTLE / Being the / History of his Peculiar Life
/ at Home and Astonishing Adventures / in Foreign
Parts. Never Before Printed. / Told by Hugh Lofting
Illustrated by the Author / [*pictures of animals, the
Doctor and characters from the book*] / Published by
Frederick A. Stokes Company at 443 Fourth Avenue,
New York. / [*flourish*] A. D. 1920 [*flourish*]

Collation: pictorial end paper showing, in silhouette, the
Doctor, palm trees, ship's mast, animals, etc., printed in purple
and light blue on off-white; half title [p. i]; blank [p. ii];
frontispiece in color, inserted; title page [p. iii]; copyright
notice [p. iv]; dedication [p. v]; blank [p. vi]; table of contents [p. vii]; blank [p. viii]; list of illustrations, pp. [ix]–x;
sub-title [p. xi]; illustration [p. xii]; text, pp. 1–180; end
paper, as described.

Bound in orange cloth stamped in light blue. Front cover
is lettered: The / [*flourishes*] Story of [*flourishes*] / Doctor
Dolittle / Hugh Lofting / [*below the author's name is pasted
a duplicate of the frontispiece trimmed to the edge of the
illustration proper and lacking the caption.*]   The sides and
bottom of the illustration are bordered by sea-creatures stamped
in light blue on the cloth. Spine is blue-stamped: The / Story
of / Doctor / Dolittle / [*short rule*] / Lofting / Stokes

All edges trimmed. Size of leaf, $8'' \times 5\frac{5}{16}''$. All illustrations as listed at pp. [ix]–x are integral parts of the text except the frontispiece and the illustrations at pp. 38 and 142.
These latter are printed on coated paper and are inserted.

1922

CARL SANDBURG

(1878–   )

ROOTABAGA / STORIES / by / Carl Sandburg /
Author of "Slabs of the Sunburnt West," "Smoke /
and Steel," "Chicago Poems," "Cornhuskers" / Illustrations and Decorations / by / Maud and Miska Peter-
sham / [*publisher's monogram*] / New York / Harcourt, Brace and Company [1922]

Collation: end paper; colored frontispiece, inserted; title
page, copyright notice on the verse dated 1922; dedication,
verso blank; table of contents, 2 leaves, verso of the last blank;
list of full page illustrations, verso blank; sub-title for the first
section [p. 1]; blank [p. 2]; text, pp. 3–230; end paper.

Bound in blue cloth with yellow stamping. The front cover
is stamped: :Rootabaga / Stories / [*decoration*] / Carl Sandburg   The spine is stamped: Rootabaga / Stories / [*rootabaga*] / Carl / Sandburg / Harcourt / Brace & Co.

All edges trimmed. Size of leaf, $7\frac{7}{8}'' \times 5\frac{3}{8}''$. All pictures
and decorations, with the exception of the frontispiece, are
integral parts of the book.

Received for copyright at the Library of Congress October
24, 1922.

1922

STEWART EDWARD WHITE

(1873–   )

DANIEL BOONE / WILDERNESS SCOUT / by /
Stewart Edward White / [*publisher's ornament in
orange printed on blind-pressed square*] / Illustrated by
/ Remington Schuyler / Garden City New York /
Doubleday, Page & Company / 1922   Enclosed by
double-rule black border; the whole enclosed by single-rule border in orange.

Collation: end paper; fly leaf; half-title with list of *Books
by Stewart Edward White* on the verso; frontispiece, inserted;
title page, with copyright notice on the verso stating: *First
Edition*; list of illustrations, verso blank; sub-title, verso blank;
text, pp. 1–308; 2 fly leaves; end paper.

Bound in blue cloth stamped in blue. Front cover is stamped:
Daniel / Boone / Wilderness / Scout / Stewart / Edward /
[*leaf*] White /   The whole is decorated by tree and mountain scene; wholly enclosed by single-rule box. Spine is
stamped: [*rule*] / Daniel / Boone / Wilderness / Scout /
[*pine-cone*] / White / Doubleday / Page & Co. / [*rule*]

All edges trimmed. Size of leaf, $7\frac{3}{8}'' \times 5''$. All illustrations
as listed are on coated paper and inserted.

Received for copyright at the Library of Congress November 18, 1922.

1923

CHARLES BOARDMAN HAWES

(1889-1923)

THE / DARK FRIGATE / Wherein is told the story
of Philip Marsham / who lived in the time of King
Charles / and was bred a sailor / but came home to
England after many hazards / by sea and land and
fought for the King at Newbury / and lost a great
inheritance and departed for Barbados / in the same
ship, by curious chance, in which / he had long before adventured / with the pirates / by / Charles
Boardman Hawes / Author of The Mutineers and the
Great Quest / [*vignette of frigate*] / Illustrated / The
Atlantic Monthy Press / Boston [1923]   Wholly
enclosed by decorative rule border.

Collation: end paper; half title, verso blank; frontispiece
on coated paper, inserted; title page, copyright notice on verso
dated 1923; dedication, verso blank; author's note regarding
his sources, verso blank; table of contents, verso blank; list
of illustrations, verso blank; sub-title [p. 1]; blank [p. 2];
text, pp. [3]–247; imprint of binder and printer [p. 248];
end paper.

Bound in vertically ribbed orange cloth stamped in black.
The front cover is lettered: The / Dark Frigate / Charles
Boardman Hawes   The lettering is above the figure of a
pistoled pirate with ship's rail, sky, etc., as background. Spine
is lettered: The / Dark / Frigate / [*rule*] / Hawes / The /
Atlantic / Monthly / Press

Top edges trimmed, other edges rough-trimmed. Size of
leaf, 8⅛" full × 5½". With the exception of the frontispiece
all other illustrations are on book paper and are integral parts
of the volume. Received for copyright at the Library of Congress November 5, 1923.

1926

WILL (WILLIAM RODERICK) JAMES

(1892–   )

SMOKY / THE COWHORSE / by / Will James /
[*vignette: horse*] / Charles Scribner's Sons / New York
[*two point-like ornaments*] London / 1926

Collation: end paper; half-title [p. i]; list of *Books by
Will James* [p. ii]; title page [p. iii]; copyright notice [p.
iv]; preface, pp. v–vi; table of contents [p. vii]; blank [p.
viii]; list of illustrations, pp. ix–xi; blank [p. xii]; sub-title
[p. xiii]; blank [p. xiv]; text, pp. 1–310; end paper.

Bound in green cloth, lettered in black. Front cover is
stamped: Smoky / by / Will James / [*horse's head printed
in dark red*]   The spine is lettered: Smoky / by / Will /
James / Scribners

Top and bottom edges trimmed, fore-edge rough-trimmed.
Size of leaf, 8″ × 5¾″. All illustrations are integral parts of
the book.

Received at the Library of Congress for copyright September
25, 1926.

A LIST OF BORDER-LINE SELECTIONS

The preceding 113 titles include all those on which there was a large measure of agreement among the librarians and collectors whose opinions were sought in making this bibliography. The following more briefly described titles include 43 well-loved books sponsored by some for a collector's list but questioned by others.

1819   IRVING, WASHINGTON.
> THE SKETCH BOOK, Part I, *New York*, 1819.
> Printed wrappers. Here included for "Rip Van Winkle" and a "Legend of Sleepy Hollow." Must have no reprint notice on wrapper or title page. For a complete list of the numerous textual points see "Washington Irving: A Bibliography," by William R. Langfeld and Philip C. Blackburn, *New York*, 1933.

1826   COOPER, JAMES FENIMORE.
> THE LAST OF THE MOHICANS, *Philadelphia*, 1826.
> 2 vols. Boards, paper label on spine. In Vol. I p. 89 is misnumbered 93. The title page of Vol. II and the blank leaf following are composed of a single sheet, inserted, folded to make four pages. This signature has been noted on both thick and thin paper but thus far no priority has been established for either type. In Vol. I p. 71 has been noted both with and without the folio; no priority established.

1839   THOMPSON, DANIEL PIERCE.
> THE GREEN MOUNTAIN BOYS, *Montpelier*, 1839.
> 2 vols. Anon. The copyright notice has been noted in two states; no known priority.

A LIST OF BORDER-LINE SELECTIONS

1840 DANA, RICHARD HENRY, JR.

TWO YEARS BEFORE THE MAST, *New York*, 1840.

Black or tan cloth. Tan cloth copies have the back cover imprinted with list of books in *Harper's Family Library*; in the first state the list does not continue beyond No. 105. Spine-stamping occurs in several states but with no known priority; number at foot of spine, when present, must be 106. Apparently several printings without change of date on title page but earliest printed copies have perfect type in the running-head at p. 9 and dotted *i* in word *in*, first line of the copyright notice.

1844-47 CHILD, LYDIA MARIA.

FLOWERS FOR CHILDREN, *New York*, 1844-45-47.

3 vols. Part I: "For Children Eight or Nine Years Old." Part II: "For Children from Four to Six Years Old." Part III: "For Children of Eleven and Twelve."

1849 PARKMAN, FRANCIS, JR.

THE CALIFORNIA AND OREGON TRAIL, *New York*, 1849.

Noted with the publisher's advertisements in two states. (A): one leaf of advertisements preceding the frontispiece and with four leaves of advertisements at the back of the book. (B): no advertisements at the front and with advertisements at the back numbered 1, 2, 3, 4, 5, 6, 8, the verso of the last leaf being blank. In *State A* the advertisements at the back are a separate signature; in *State B* the advertisements are part of the final signature. Study of type-wear indicates that *State A* was first printed and the copy at the Library of Congress, although lacking all advertisements (possibly extracted since the volume is rebound) has the final signature of text as of *State A*. James E. Walsh in *The New Colophon*, N. Y., 1950, ("The California and Oregon Trail: A Bibliographical Study") confirms the priority of *State A*.

1856 CRANCH, CHRISTOPHER PEARSE.

THE LAST OF THE HUGGERMUGGERS, *Boston*, 1856.

A LIST OF BORDER-LINE SELECTIONS

1867 MITCHELL, S. WEIR.
THE WONDERFUL STORIES OF FUZ-BUZ THE FLY AND
MOTHER GRABEM THE SPIDER, *Philadelphia,* 1867.
Anonymous.

1870 DIAZ, ABBY MORTON.
THE WILLIAM HENRY LETTERS, *Boston,* 1870.

1870 PHELPS, ELIZABETH STUART.
THE TROTTY BOOK, *Boston,* 1870.

1876 TAYLOR, BAYARD.
BOYS OF OTHER COUNTRIES, *New York,* 1876.

1878 WARNER, CHARLES DUDLEY.
BEING A BOY, *Boston,* 1878.
In the publisher's advertisements facing the title page the
present title is described as *just ready.*

1881 LANIER, SIDNEY.
THE BOY'S MABINOGION, *New York,* 1881.

1884 JACKSON, HELEN HUNT.
RAMONA, *Boston,* 1884.

1885 CUSTER, ELIZABETH B.
"BOOTS AND SADDLES," *New York,* 1885.

1888 COBB, SYLVANUS, JR.
THE GUNMAKER OF MOSCOW, *New York* [1888].
Argument exists as to the first edition. The author's
daughter stated that the book was first published with
the Cassell imprint and *Publishers' Weekly,* October 20,
1888, records receipt of a copy with the Cassell imprint.
The same magazine reports receipt of the Bonner
imprint on May 18th, 1889.

1890 JANVIER, THOMAS A.
THE AZTEC TREASURE HOUSE, *New York,* 1890.

1890 OGDEN, RUTH.
A LOYAL LITTLE RED-COAT, *New York,* 1890.

A LIST OF BORDER-LINE SELECTIONS

1892 FRANCIS, J. G.
A BOOK OF CHEERFUL CATS AND OTHER ANIMATED
ANIMALS, *New York*, 1892.

1895 SMITH, GERTRUDE.
THE ARABELLA AND ARAMINTA STORIES, *Boston*, 1895.
Also 15 de luxe copies signed by author and illustrator.

1896 STEARNS, ALBERT.
SINBAD SMITH & CO., *New York*, 1896.

1897 CARRUTH, HAYDEN.
THE VOYAGE OF THE RATTLETRAP, *New York*, 1897.

1897 WATERLOO, STANLEY.
THE STORY OF AB, *Chicago*, 1897.

1898 HUGHES, RUPERT.
THE LAKERIM ATHLETIC CLUB, *New York*, 1898.

1903 ADAMS, ANDY.
THE LOG OF A COWBOY, *Boston*, 1903.

1903 FOX, JOHN, JR.
THE LITTLE SHEPHERD OF KINGDOM COME, *New York*,
1903.
First state has *laugh* for *lap*, p. 61, line 14. A few copies
have been noted in unstamped red cloth, paper label
on spine, edges untrimmed. Since one of the latter
state has been noted with a presentation inscription
by the author it is assumed that such copies were
intended for his personal use. The first state of the
trade edition has no advertisements on the verso of
the half title. In addition to the trade edition the
publishers issued an advance state in red boards,
paper label, with sheets printed from the magazine
plates.

1904 PIER, ARTHUR STANWOOD.
BOYS OF ST. TIMOTHY'S, *New York*, 1904.
Published September, 1904 on copyright page.

1904 PORTER, GENE STRATTON.
FRECKLES, *New York*, 1904.

A LIST OF BORDER-LINE SELECTIONS

1905 HAMMOND, HAROLD.
PINKEY PERKINS: JUST A BOY, *New York,* 1905.

1906 DIX, BEULAH MARIE.
MERRYLIPS, *New York,* 1906.

1907 ALTSHELER, JOSEPH A.
THE YOUNG TRAILERS, *New York,* 1907.

1909 MUIR, JOHN.
STICKEEN, *Boston,* 1909.

1910 BURGESS, THORNTON W.
OLD MOTHER WEST WIND, *Boston* [1910].

1911 PERKINS, LUCY FITCH.
THE DUTCH TWINS, *Boston,* 1911.

1912 ATKINSON, ELEANOR.
GREYFRIARS BOBBY, *New York,* 1912.
First printing does not have the publisher's code letters
    on the copyright page and states: *Published Feb-*
    ruary, 1912.

1912 KNIPE, EMILIE BENSON, AND ARTHUR AL-
    DEN KNIPE.
THE LUCKY SIXPENCE, *New York,* 1912.

1913 PEARSON, EDMUND L.
THE VOYAGE OF THE HOPPERGRASS, *New York,* 1913.

1915 KNEELAND, CLARISSA A.
SMUGGLER'S ISLAND AND THE DEVIL FIRES OF SAN
    MOROS, *Boston,* 1915.

1915 SABIN, EDWIN L.
THE GOLD SEEKERS OF '49, *Philadelphia,* 1915.

1919 TERHUNE, ALBERT PAYSON.
LAD: A DOG, *New York* [1919].

1921 VAN LOON, HENDRIK WILLEM.
THE STORY OF MANKIND [*New York*] 1921.

1929 FIELD, RACHEL.
HITTY: HER FIRST HUNDRED YEARS, *New York,* 1929.

INDEX

Abbott, Jacob, 2-3
Adams, Andy, 146
Adams, William T., 12
Admiral's Caravan, The, 96
Adventures of Huckleberry Finn, The, 75-76
Adventures of Tom Sawyer, The, 43-44
Age of Chivalry, The, 14-15
Age of Fable, The, 13
Alcott, Louisa May, 30, 33-34, 36
Alden, Isabella MacDonald, 22
Aldrich, Thomas Bailey, 35
Alger, Horatio, Jr., 29, 37
Altsheler, Joseph A., 147
American Boys Handy Book, The, 62
Andrews, Jane, 18, 79
Anne of Green Gables, 124
Arabella and Araminta Stories, The, 146
Atkinson, Eleanor, 147
Aztec Treasure House, The, 145

Baldwin, James, 63, 85
Barbour, Ralph Henry, 108
Barnaby Lee, 116
Barnum, Frances Courtenay Baylor, 90
Barr, Amelia E., 82
Baum, L. Frank, 111-113
Baylor, Frances Courtenay, 90
Beard, Daniel (Dan) Carter, 62
Beautiful Joe, 100-101
Being a Boy, 145
Bennett, John, 104, 116
Betty Leicester, 93
Birds' Christmas Carol, The, 86
Boat Club, The, 12
Bodley Family, The, in Town and Country, 41-42

Book of Cheerful Cats, A, 146
"*Boots and Saddles,*" 145
Bow of Orange Ribbon, The, 82
Boy Emigrants, The, 48-49
Boy Travellers in the Far East, The, 53
Boys' Mabinogion, The, 145
Boys of Other Countries, 145
Boys of St. Timothy's, The, 146
Boys of '76, The, 47
Boy's Town, A, 92
Brooks, Noah, 48-49
Brownies, The, 84
Bulfinch, Thomas, 13, 14-15
Burgess, Gelett, 110
Burgess, Thornton W., 147
Burnett, Frances Hodgson, 80-81, 88
Burroughs, Edgar Rice, 134
Butterworth, Hezekiah, 50-51

Cadet Days, 98
Calhoun, Frances Boyd, 127
California and Oregon Trail, The, 144
Call of the Wild, The, 119-120
Canfield, Dorothy, 137
Captain January, 94
"*Carleton,*" 47
Carruth, Hayden, 146
Carryl, Charles E., 77-78, 96
Castlemon, Harry, 27
Champney, Lizzie W., 69-70
Child, Lydia Maria, 144
Clarke, Rebecca Sophia, 21, 23
Clemens, Samuel L., 43-44, 65-66, 75-76
Cobb, Sylvanus, 145
Coffin, Charles Carleton, 47
Coolidge, Susan, 39
Cooper, James Fenimore, 143

INDEX

Court of Boyville, The, 109
Cox, Palmer, 84
Cranch, Christopher Pearse, 144
Cudjo's Cave, 20
Cummins, Maria S., 11
Custer, Elizabeth B., 145

Daddy-Long-Legs, 130
Dana, Richard Henry, 144
Daniel Boone: Wilderness Scout,
  140
Dark Frigate, The, 141
Davy and the Goblin, 77-78
Diaz, Abby Morton, 145
Diddie, Dumps and Tot, 64
Dix, Beulah Marie, 147
Doctor Dolittle, The Story of, 138
Dodge, Mary Mapes, 25
Doings of the Bodley Family in
  Town and Country, 41-42
Dotty Dimple, 23
Du Chaillu, Paul, 28
Dutch Twins, The, 147

Editha's Burglar, 88
Eggleston, Edward, 71-72
Ellis, Edward S., 16-17
Elsie Dinsmore, 26

Faith Gartney's Girlhood, 19
Family Flight . . . , A, 58
Farquharson, Martha, 26
Field, Rachel, 147
Finley, Martha, 26
Five Little Peppers and How They
  Grew, 54-55
Flamingo Feather, The, 83
Floating Prince, The, 61
Flight of Pony Baker, The, 117
Flowers for Children, 144
Fosdick, Charles Austin, 27
Fox, John, Jr., 146
Francis, Joseph Greene, 146

Frank on the Lower Mississippi,
  27
Freckles, 146
Fur-Seal's Tooth, The, 102
Fuz-Buz the Fly, 145

Gold Seekers of '49, The, 147
Goodrich, S. G., 1
Goops and How to Be Them, 110
Goulding, F. R., 9
Grant, Robert, 87
Green Mountain Boys, The, 143
Greyfriars Bobby, 147
Gunmaker of Moscow, The, 145

Habberton, John, 45-46
Hale, Edward Everett, 24, 58
Hale, Lucretia P., 52
Hale, Susan, 58
Half-Back, The, 108
Hammond, Harold, 147
Hans Brinker, 25
Harris, Joel Chandler, 56-57
Hawes, Charles Boardman, 141
Hawthorne, Nathaniel, 6, 10
Hegan, Alice Caldwell, 114
Helen Lester, 22
Helen's Babies, 45-46
Hitty, 147
Hole Book, The, 125
Hollow Tree, The, 105
Hoosier School-Boy, The, 71-72
Hough, Emerson, 126
Howells, William Dean, 92, 117
Huckleberry Finn, 75-76
Hughes, Rupert, 146

Irving, Washington, 143

Jack Hall, 87
Jack Hazard and His Fortunes, 38
Jackson, Helen Hunt, 145
James, Will, 142
Janvier, Thomas A., 145
Jenny Wren's Boarding House, 97

150

INDEX

Jewett, Sarah Orne, 93
Johnson, Owen, 128, 129
Johnson, Rossiter, 60
Johnston, Annie Fellows, 103
Juan and Juanita, 90

Kaler, James Otis, 59, 97
Kellogg, Elijah, 31
King, Charles, 98
Kneeland, Clarissa, 147
Knipe, Arthur Alden, 147
Knipe, Emilie Benson, 147
Knox, Thomas W., 53

Lad: A Dog, 147
Lakerim Athletic Club, The, 146
Lamplighter, The, 11
Lanier, Sidney, 145
Last of the Huggermuggers, The, 144
Last of the Mohicans, The, 143
Lion Ben of Elm Island, 31
Little Colonel, The, 103
Little Lord Fauntleroy, 80-81
Little Men, 36
Little Prudy, 21
Little Shepherd of Kingdom Come, The, 146
Little Smoke, 95
Little Women, 30
Lofting, Hugh, 138
Log of a Cowboy, The, 146
London, Jack, 119-120, 122-123
Lothrop, Harriet Mulford Stone, 54-55
Loyal Little Red-Coat, A, 145
Lucky Sixpence, The, 147

Man Without a Country, The, 24
Marshall, Margaret, 100
Master Skylark, 104
May, Sophie, 21, 23
Merry Adventures of Robin Hood, The, 73
Merrylips, 147

Miss Minerva and William Green Hill, 127
Mitchell, S. Weir, 145
Montgomery, L. M., 124
Mrs. Wiggs of the Cabbage Patch, 114
Muir, John, 147
Munroe, Kirk, 83, 102

Newell, Peter, 125

Ogden, Ruth, 145
Old-Fashioned Girl, An, 33-34
Old Mother West Wind, 147
Optic, Oliver, 12
Oregon Trail, The, 144
Otis, James, 59, 97
Otto of the Silver Hand, 91

Page, Thomas Nelson, 89
Paine, Albert Bigelow, 105
Pansy, 22
Parkman, Francis, 144
Parley, Peter, 1
Pearson, Edmund L., 147
Peary, Josephine Diebitsch, 115
Peck, George W., 67-68
Peck's Bad Boy and His Pa, 67-68
Penrod, 132-133
Penrod and Sam, 135-136
Perkins, Lucy Fitch, 147
Peter Parley, 1
Peterkin Papers, The, 52
Phaeton Rogers, 60
Phelps, Elizabeth Stuart, 145
Pier, Arthur Stanwood, 146
Pinkey Perkins, 147
Pollyanna, 131
Porter, Eleanor H., 131
Porter, Gene Stratton, 146
Prince and the Pauper, The, 65-66
Pyle, Howard, 73, 91
Pyrnelle, Louise-Clarke, 64

INDEX

Queechy, 7-8

Ragged Dick, 29
Ramona, 145
Rebecca of Sunnybrook Farm, 121
Real Diary of a Real Boy, The, 118
Rice, Alice Caldwell Hegan, 114
Richards, Laura E., 94
Robert and Harold; or, The Young Marooners, 9
Robin Hood, 73
Rollo, 2-3
Rootabaga Stories, 139

Sabin, Edwin L., 147
Sandburg, Carl, 139
Saunders, Marshall, 100-101
Scudder, Horace E., 41
Search for Andrew Field, The, 99
Seth Jones, 16-17
Seton, Ernest Thompson, 106-107
Seven Little Sisters, 18
Shute, Henry A., 118
Sidney, Margaret, 54-55
Sinbad Smith & Co., 146
Sketch Book, The, 143
Smith, Gertrude, 146
Smoky, The Cowhorse, 142
Smuggler's Island, 147
Snow Baby, The, 115
Stearns, Albert, 146
Stephens, Charles A., 40
Stickeen, 147
Stockton, Frank R., 32, 61
Stoddard, William O., 95
Stories of the Gorilla Country, 28
Story of a Bad Boy, The, 35
Story of Ab, The, 146
Story of Doctor Dolittle, The, 138
Story of Mankind, The, 147
Story of Siegfried, The, 63
Story of the Golden Age, A, 85

Tales of Peter Parley About America, The, 1
Tanglewood Tales, 10
Tarkington, Booth, 132-133, 135-136
Tarzan of the Apes, 134
Tattered Tom, 37
Taylor, Bayard, 145
Ten Boys Who Lived on the Road, 79
Tennessee Shad, The, 129
Terhune, Albert Payson, 147
Thompson, Daniel P., 143
Thompson, Ernest Seton, 106-107
Three Vassar Girls Abroad, 69-70
Ting a Ling, 32
Toby Tyler, 59
Tom Sawyer, 43-44
Tomlinson, Everett T., 99
Trotty Book, The, 145
Trowbridge, John Townsend, 20, 38
Twain, Mark, 43-44, 65-66, 75-76
Two Little Confederates, 89
Two Years Before the Mast, 144

Uncle Remus: His Songs and His Sayings, 56-57
Understood Betsy, 137

Van Loon, Hendrik Willem, 147
Varmint, The, 128
Voyage of the Hoppergrass, The, 147
Voyage of the Rattletrap, The, 146

Warner, Charles Dudley, 145
Warner, Susan, 4-5, 7-8
Waterloo, Stanley, 146
Webster, Jean, 130
Wetherell, Elizabeth, 4-5, 7-8
What Katy Did, 39

INDEX

White Fang, 122-123
White, Stewart Edward, 140
White, William Allen, 109
Whitney, A. D. T., 19
Wide, Wide World, The, 4-5
Wiggin, Kate Douglas, 86, 121
Wild Animals I Have Known,
  106-107
William Henry Letters, The, 145
Wizard of Oz, The Wonderful,
  111-113
Wonder-Book for Girls and Boys,
  A, 6

Wonderful Stories of Fuz-Buz the
  Fly and Mother Grabem the
  Spider, 145
Wonderful Wizard of Oz, The,
  111-113
Woolsey, Sara Chauncey, 39

Young Alaskans, The, 126
Young Marooners, The, 9
Young Moose Hunters, The, 40
Young Trailers, The, 147

Zigzag Journeys in Europe, 50-51